DUCKWORTH CLASSICAL ESSAYS

Interpreting Classical Texts

Malcolm Heath

Duckworth

This impression 2007
First published in 2002 by
Gerald Duckworth & Co. Ltd.
90-93 Cowcross Street, London EC1M 6BF
Tel: 020 7490 7300
Fax: 020 7490 0080
inquiries@duckworth-publishers.co.uk
www.ducknet.co.uk

A catalogue record for this book is available
from the British Library

ISBN-10: 0 7156 3174 8
ISBN-13: 9780715631744

Typeset by Ray Davies
Printed and bound in Great Britain by
CPI Antony Rowe, Eastbourne

Interpreting Classical Texts

Contents

Contents

Preface

When I started working on a doctoral thesis on Greek tragedy in 1980, it seemed obvious to me that I should devote a significant proportion of my time and effort to thinking systematically about what I was trying to do. The eccentricity of this idea (at the time, Classics at Oxford was not a hotbed of literary theory) carried through into my conclusions: an interpretative project that was intentionalist (but not like Hirsch) and reception-theoretical (but not like Jauss), set in the context of a larger framework that viewed the diversity of interpretative projects in a critically (but not syncretistically) pluralist light, and underpinned by an approach to enquiry that was hermeneutic (but not like Gadamer) and pragmatist (but not like Rorty), and by an approach to language that did not see Saussure as a fruitful starting-point, and therefore had no interest in the games that could be played with his deconstructed remains. Since then my thinking has developed in the light of further reflection, further reading, further experience of research and a consequent engagement with different research questions. But I am still eccentric enough to find the conclusions I reached then in substance valid. They have provided the largely implicit theoretical rationale for all my subsequent work, and this book aims to make explicit, in outline, the current state of my thinking on that rationale.

In the intervening years my research has developed in a number of wholly unexpected directions, and has taken me to destinations a long way from tragedy. Readers should note, therefore, that 'classical' is used in this book as a shorthand reference to Greco-Roman antiquity, conceived in broad terms chronologically and without any limitation to a literary canon.

I have been intending to write this book, or something like it, for a long time. I am grateful to Tom Harrison, who at an opportune moment provided the impetus to convert the design or plan in the author's mind into intentional action. I am also grateful, for reasons that will become clear in Chapter 1, to all those scholars with whose views I take issue; Don Fowler, whose acute and provocative intelligence is sadly missed, deserves a special mention here. Roger Brock offered encouragement and epigraphic advice. David Levene displayed uncanny penetration in identifying errors, ambiguities and other defects in the penultimate draft; if I have failed to correct (or disguise) them, he is not to blame. Carol Poster would be an ecological disaster if questions were a non-renewable resource; I have derived unfailing stimulus, challenge and enjoyment from our wide-ranging discussions.

University of Leeds   M.H.
July 2002

1

Interpretation and dissent

How should I interpret a classical text? However I interpret it, someone else will interpret it differently. Disagreement is endemic to the field. Let us begin by taking stock of this fact, and exploring its implications.

1.1. Disagreement

By the end of Sophocles' *Antigone* it is clear that Creon made a bad mistake when he banned the burial of Polynices' body. That decision has led to the deaths of his niece, son and wife; Creon's life is in ruins. But at what point does it become clear that he has made a mistake? As I read the play, it is clear from the very start. After all, the exposure of a corpse is an ethically and emotionally charged act, and in tragedy it should not need much to alert us to the possibility of an error of judgement that will have disastrous consequences.[1] Most interpreters, however, would reject this point of view, finding instead a process of gradual disclosure. That interpretation is not by any means an arbitrary or irrational one; there are arguments that can be made in support of it. Those arguments are not, in my judgement, compelling – at any rate, they have not yet persuaded me to change my mind on the main point. Even so, I have learned a great deal from interpreters whose reading of the play conflicts with mine. Their work often draws attention to features of the text that I had overlooked or failed to take adequately into account. For example, they have helped me to see that I once gave too little weight to the negative aspects of Antigone's defiance in the context of Greek attitudes to women acting independently. To sustain my overall interpretation, therefore, I have had to adjust it in detail in the light of conflicting readings of the play. The arguments I advance in favour of my own interpretation might in turn have a similar influence on others.

Interpreters who hold conflicting views may therefore influence each other through discussion, and this mutual influence may result in a convergence of opinion on many individual points even if it does not lead to overall consensus. Indeed, the process may make overall consensus more difficult to achieve. As interpreters learn from each other they refine their interpretations, making them richer, more subtly nuanced, more comprehensive in their treatment of the evidence – and thus more resilient and more robust. Paradoxically, convergence in detail may in this way serve to entrench global disagreement. And there is no reason to believe that this is a temporary phenomenon. People have been discussing *Antigone* for a long time without achieving a stable consensus: why should that change now? The focus of scholarly disagreement may move over time, but the fact of disagreement does not go away. It is our constant, if migratory, companion.

How should we respond to this situation? We might react despondently (if we can never reach agreement, isn't the enterprise of interpretation futile?) or with elation (liberated from the tyranny of the One True Meaning, interpreters are free to do whatever they want). Or we might simply ask why a failure to achieve consensus should be thought to *need* a response. Consensus *as such* has no intrinsic value: consensus may be consensus in error. We will not gain anything from reaching a consensus that the fungi before us are delicious mushrooms if they are poisonous toadstools. If we are fallible (as we are), then any stable consensus is likely to be, in some measure, a stable consensus in error. So the absence of disagreement should not necessarily be seen as a mark of success: it may be a symptom of uncritical acquiescence in prevailing dogma. Conversely, disagreement ought not to be seen as a mark of failure; instead, it should be welcomed as a safeguard against complacent persistence in error. Dissent has a positive value. It is an integral part of the dynamic that drives enquiry forward.

1.2. Reflection

The fact of disagreement merits further examination. When I say that in *Antigone* Creon's error of judgement is clear from the outset, what exactly am I claiming? That it is clear to me? That it should be clear to everyone? That it would have been clear to Sophocles' original audience? That Sophocles meant it to be clear? This list of possibilities is not exhaustive. Apparently, there are many different claims that could be made using the same form of words.

Among the claims that *I* want to make are that (probably) Sophocles meant Creon's error of judgement to be clear from the outset, and that (probably) it would have been clear from the outset to Sophocles' original audience. (That is, of course, a generalisation, and is not meant to exclude the possibility that there were members of the audience – obviously not a wholly uniform entity – who reacted in other ways.)

Creon's error of judgement is also, in a sense, clear to me. But that was not always the case. It only became clear to me when I began to pursue questions about Sophocles' (probable) intentions and the (probable) reaction of his audience in the context of a developing theory about the nature of Greek tragedy. So if I were to say that it is clear to me, that would not really add anything to the claims about Sophocles and his audience already stated. I would simply be saying that it is clear to me that these are the answers to the questions I am asking about Sophocles and his audience. This is not a very strong, and not a very interesting, assertion. It means only that I am currently unable to organise the data in any other way and still find the result equally convincing. (Clarity is not the same as certainty – not even if *I* am certain, in the sense of feeling a high level of confidence. Many things that used to be clear to me now seem clearly wrong, and I have no doubt that I will change my mind on many things that are clear to me now. The need for a standing acknowledgement of fallibility is a theme that will recur in this and subsequent chapters.) The relevant claims, then, are those that I wish to make about Sophocles and his audience.

Let us now consider a reader who *denies* that Creon's error is apparent from the outset. In her view, Creon's edict seems statesmanlike and patriotic at first, and the error of judgement is only gradually disclosed as the play progresses. If this reader is making a claim about what Sophocles meant or how his audience would have reacted, then she is disagreeing with me. But if she is not making a claim about Sophocles or his audience, it may be that there is no disagreement between us. Giving a different answer to a different question involves no contradiction.

If we probe more deeply, however, we may well find disagreement after all. Consider a hypothetical case. Alan accepts my view that Sophocles meant Creon's error to be clear from the outset, while Barbara maintains that Sophocles' audience would have found Creon's edict statesmanlike and patriotic at first. There is no direct contradiction between these two positions, since they are answers to different questions. But it is unlikely that either interpreter will find the other's interpretation a plausible answer even to the question that the other is posing. If both interpretations are right, a highly successful dramatist badly misjudged the reaction of a familiar audience whose culture he shared. That is, of course, possible, but neither Alan nor Barbara think it at all likely. (Nor do I, which is why, in my own interpretation, claims about Sophocles and about his audience are correlated with each other. That assumes, obviously, that Greek tragedians were writing at least in part to be understood by audiences in the contemporary theatre. I think there are good reasons for accepting this assumption – which should not be taken to imply that I would wish to generalise it to cover all authors in all circumstances.) So the answers which Alan and Barbara give to their respective questions, though not in a strict sense contradictory, sit uneasily together. The divergence between them is likely to be symptomatic of underlying disagreements on many points of detail.

Let us suppose that Barbara's hypothesis about the reaction of Sophocles' audience rests on (among other things) the fact that Athenian law forbade burial to traitors; an Athenian audience would therefore, she contends, have had some sympathy with Creon's treatment of the traitor Polynices. Alan, previously unaware of this law, recognises its relevance; but he concludes after reflection that the Athenian prohibition, which allowed burial outside the bounds of native territory, is crucially different from Creon's insistence on leaving a corpse exposed within the bounds of native territory. He therefore sees no reason to abandon his original position. But it does occur to him that he now has a solution to a problem whose force he had not properly appreciated before: if Creon's edict is seriously and evidently misguided, will he not appear stupid or depraved? What Alan has just learned about Athenian law suggests a way in which the edict could be seen as an error of judgement that an intelligent, statesmanlike and patriotic man might plausibly make in a crisis. So detailed adjustments can be made to Alan's overall position that render it more complex and comprehensive. For him, the disagreement has been fruitful.

Of course, Alan could have reached the same conclusion by other routes. He could have come across a reference to the Athenian law in some quite different context, noticed its relevance to *Antigone*, and examined its implications. Or perhaps he already knew about the Athenian law; in that case, a realisation that it posed a possible threat to his interpretation of the play could have prompted him to examine its implications. Or he might have become uneasy at the implication in his reading of the play that Creon must have been stupid or depraved, and have come across (or remembered about) the Athenian penalty for traitors as he reflected on this problem. In these last two cases Alan becomes dissatisfied with his current understanding of *Antigone* (in the first case he sees a possible inconsistency with other information in his possession, in the second he sees a problem which his current understanding fails to address); it is this dissatisfaction that provides the stimulus for further enquiry. His self-critical stance – his willingness to recognise and address possible weaknesses in his own interpretation – results in a process of internalised disagreement. Dialogue with others extends this process into another, more public dimension.

Barbara, for her part, concedes Alan's point that the Athenian law is different from Creon's edict in an important respect. So perhaps she will abandon her view of the original audience's probable reaction – or, very likely, she will not. And reasonably so: conceding Alan's point does not require her to attach the same weight to it as he does. An interpretation is not a heap of isolated propositions, but a network of interrelated propositions. When we adopt a new proposition, the network is changed. But the influence is reciprocal: a newly adopted proposition has to be integrated into that existing network, and *how* it is integrated depends in part on the network's prior shape. A new item of information therefore does not carry its significance around with it: it *gains* significance from the relations established with information that we already hold. This means that the 'same' information may have a different significance for different interpreters, and lead them to conflicting conclusions.

That is one of the reasons why disagreement is unlikely ever to be eradicated. It is also a reason why the public dimension of disagreement is important. Because other interpreters integrate information into different networks, and so are likely to attach a different significance to it, engaging with their interpretations can open our eyes to a range of possible alternatives to our current views more diverse and more far-reaching – more global in their implications – than any we are likely to think up for ourselves. Alan's self-critical stance can be made more rigorous and more creative if it draws on the criticisms that are implicit in the conflicting views of others, or explicit in their objections to his own.

Now that Alan has come to appreciate the potential value of other people's objections, the time has come to expose him to a more radical critique. Charles has been waiting patiently to explain why Alan's interpretation of *Antigone* is illegitimate in principle. Alan wishes to make a claim about Sophocles' intentions. But Charles, in agreement with influential trends in modern critical thought, maintains that authors' intentions are both irrelevant and irrecoverable. If that is right, then Alan is not just saying the wrong thing about the play; he is saying the wrong *kind* of thing. The fact that we disagree about the answers to our questions may seem trivial in the face of disagreement about which questions we should ask. We need to move the discussion to another plane.

1.3. Theory

How should I interpret a classical text? Reflectively. First, we need to reflect on our interpretations – on the answers we give to our questions – in order to achieve the self-critical stance commended in the previous section. Secondly, we need to reflect on our questions. We need to understand what we are doing, not least to avoid talking at fruitlessly crossed purposes when we happen to be doing different things. The discovery that there may be disagreement about what we *should* be doing only adds urgency to that need.

Challenges to the legitimacy of a particular category of question point us to one level of reflection. In order to respond to such challenges (to determine, for example, whether it is true that someone who asks questions about authorial intention is trying to say the wrong kind of thing about a literary text) we must be able to *evaluate* questions. That is one possible level of reflection. But we cannot evaluate questions unless we understand them and their implications. What (for example) do we mean by 'intention'? If we ask what Sophocles intended, what are we actually asking for? This quest for *clarification* is a second possible level of reflection. We can also, thirdly, reflect on *methodology*: given that I am asking *this* question, how might I go about answering it? If I persist in asking questions about Sophocles' intentions, what kinds of evidence would be relevant to identifying those intentions? Of course, methodological reflection is also underpinned by the quest for clarification: we cannot hope to determine the best way to do something unless we understand what it is we are trying to do.

If we attempt to clarify, evaluate and methodologically orient our interpretative questions, we are engaged in various kinds of *theoretical* thinking. My call for reflective interpretation is, therefore, in part, a claim that interpreters of classical texts are under an obligation to engage in theory. But we must be realistic about what can be expected from that engagement. Our move to the level of theory began when we encountered a disagreement about the kinds of question that interpreters should ask, but there is no presumption that the move will resolve the disagreement. On the contrary, theory is itself a locus of disagreement, as a glance at recent theoretical writing will readily confirm; and there is no greater prospect of achieving stable consensus at this level than there was when we focussed on the texts alone.

Perhaps, then, the proposed detour through theory is a pointless diversion; perhaps we should resist the distraction, and return to the texts. Such a conclusion would certainly appeal to those classicists who take, or appear to take, an anti-theoretical stance. But appearance may deceive. We should take note, first, of a possible ambiguity in the word 'theory'. I have been using it to designate open reflection on the interpreter's task, but it is also and often used pre-emptively to designate a range of favoured theories. For example: 'The term "literary theory" is roughly synonymous with discussions of Nietzsche, Freud, Heidegger, Derrida, Lacan, Foucault, de Man, Lyotard, *et al.*'[2] It might be argued that this tendentious usage, to the extent that it tends to foreclose theoretical reflection by tacitly excluding whatever falls outside the favoured range, is an obstacle to reflection, and is thus itself more genuinely anti-theoretical than the apparent hostility to theory that it often evokes. Likewise, there are those whose hostility to theory is based on what they perceive (rightly or wrongly) as the systematic obscurity of much 'theoretical' writing, and its questionable standards of argument. Such a position, too, might be construed as a rejection of anti-theoretical tendencies in 'theory', rather than a rejection of theory as such.

Resistance to 'theory' is therefore not necessarily resistance to the kind of theoretical reflection that I have urged, and classicists who appear to take an anti-theoretical stance need not be denying that interpretation should be undertaken reflectively. It might, after all, be thought to go without saying that we should try to understand what we are doing. Responsible scholarship incurs certain obligations, including the obligations of clarity and rigour. We *ought* to be clear about what we are trying to achieve, and how we might reasonably try to achieve it; we *ought* to be able to give an account of and to justify our practice. How else are we to engage in rational discussion of our disagreements in these matters? The alternative is irresponsible dogmatism. Thus the move to the level of theory should not be seen as resolving our disagreements, so much as improving the quality of the debates they prompt.

However, the theoretical examination of interpretative procedures must be curtailed at some point: *exhaustive* reflection is impossible. And it seems unlikely that any interpreter is *wholly* unreflective. So there is really no point in trying to give a generalised verdict for theory or against. We face a more modest task: assessing the potential benefits of a given investment of time and effort in theoretical reflection rather than in the practice of interpretation. Whenever we are invited to take a theoretical detour, it is open to us to decide that there are other, more profitable, ways to use our time and effort.

A minimalist stance towards theory could even lay claim to a theoretical rationale. Interpreting is a basic human activity. Human beings are, for the most part, thoroughly trained interpreters, because human existence is social. It is impossible for us to flourish without achieving some large measure of communicative success, which in turn depends on understanding others and correctly anticipating their capacity to understand us. Social interaction therefore compels us to be interpreters, and provides a constant stream of feedback that trains us in the skills of interpretation. The exercise of these skills is largely tacit; we do not need to think about them, any more than we need to think about how to walk or catch a ball. In everyday life, therefore, interpretation is typically unreflective. If theoretical reflection simply reaffirms the tacit skills we have acquired in this way, it adds nothing; if it contradicts them, that is probably evidence that the theory is flawed. For we have compelling empirical reason to think that human beings are good interpreters, and very little reason to think that they are good at constructing abstract theories of interpretation.

It is true and important that interpretation is always rooted in the tacit skills that are acquired through social interaction. Nevertheless, the minimalist argument I have just sketched does not exhaust the possible contribution of theory. Even if theory left everything as it was, merely making explicit a tacit skill, it might still have a function in countering the distorting influences of *bad* theory. Theory may be therapeutic. More positively, the texts that classicists deal with are often very complex, and are always culturally distanced from us. This fact, together with the limited and fragmentary state of the evidence on which we depend, means that we cannot rely on the rich shared cognitive environment that underpins interpretation in ordinary social intercourse. When we try to interpret complex and culturally alien texts we engage in an activity that may be continuous with what we do day-to-day, but is not by any means identical with it. That is why the question with which this chapter opened seems a reasonable one to ask: when we start to look hard at classical texts, we encounter problems that we do not already know how to handle. So perhaps reflection is necessary, after all. Furthermore, we have seen that there are many different questions that can be asked. Theoretical reflection may prompt us to see that there are kinds of questions worth asking which do not arise in day-to-day interpretation.

I believe, then, that the classicist should see interpretation and theory as interdependent activities. But the interdependence is not symmetrical. Interpretation without theoretical reflection may be limited in scope and is vulnerable to various kinds of muddle; that certainly makes it worth less. But theory that is not rooted in our existing interpretative skills is at risk of being vacuous speculation; and that would make it worthless.

1.4. Philosophy

The issues that arise in theoretical discussion are, in part, issues of the kind traditionally addressed by philosophers. We have, then, to reckon with another shift of level: theoretical discussion leads to an engagement with philosophy, just as interpretative discussion led to reflection and thus to an engagement with theory.

We should not expect this shift of level to furnish us with any resolution to our disagreements, either. After all, debating philosophical issues has conspicuously failed to furnish philosophers with a resolution to *their* disagreements. All that philosophy can do is enlarge still further the field across which our disagreements range. This is not at all to say that the recourse to philosophy is pointless. I have argued that disagreement has a positive value, and that there is a potential qualitative gain from the enlargement of our disagreements through theoretical reflection; the same applies here. But so, too, does the observation that we need to make a realistic assessment of what we stand to gain from the investment of time and effort in enquiry at a certain level of abstraction, and what we stand to lose by the diversion of time and effort from more concrete interpretative activity.

One point that needs to be considered in making that assessment is what practical difference a decision between competing philosophical positions would make. The bearing of philosophy on practice is often very limited. Two philosophers who hold radically different philosophies of language are still able to talk to each other. Their ability to use and understand language derives from the kind of tacit interpretative skill we mentioned in the last section, and is independent of their philosophies. It does not follow from this that we should not pursue theoretical issues to the philosophical level. If nothing else, it may, like theory, be useful therapeutically; that is, it may offer a defence against the effects of bad, or misapplied, philosophy. And it may, positively, help us achieve a better understanding of the problems we encounter at less abstract levels of reflection. But we should not think of this move as leading to the subordination of theory (or of interpretative practice) to a superior wisdom.

1. *Interpretation and dissent*

We may pursue this line of thought in connection with what Don Fowler, under the influence of the neo-pragmatist philosopher Richard Rorty, calls 'anti-foundationalism'. Consider the following remarks:[3]

> Naturally, in the end my reading is my reading, based on the stories I want to tell. I should like to convince others of it and them, and to argue: I should like to be forced to modify elements of my position, to be brought to see things I have missed. But it's no good pretending that I didn't *make it all up*. Can we believe a critic who tells us this? Can we admit what we are doing, but take it seriously? I would argue that the answer is again 'yes'. And again, it seems to me particularly curious that classical scholars of all people should be determined to situate their stories so firmly 'out there' when even the most apparently objective features of their texts are up for grabs.

Fowler contrasts a recognition that one is telling stories that one has made up with a pretence that the stories one is telling are 'out there'. Let us begin with that last phrase – noting first that the quotation marks are not signalling a quotation (one would be hard put to find many classical scholars who have characterised their work in these words); this is Fowler's own expression. So what might it mean to 'situate their stories ... "out there" '? Out where? Imagine a philosophy seminar interrupted by a fire alarm. We will not be perplexed if a student asks, 'Is there a fire out there?' They would be asking (presumably) whether the alarm is one genuinely triggered by a fire in some other part of the building, or whether it is a false alarm. But what would we make of the question, 'Is there a fire "out there"?' Perhaps we could read it as a gesture towards issues concerning metaphysical realism: is the fire a reality that exists independently of our knowledge of it? The answer we give to a question of that kind does not have any bearing on the answer to the former question. There may be a fire out there, whether or not there is a fire 'out there'. (This is one reason why starting a discussion of metaphysical realism would be such an untimely response to the fire-alarm. By contrast, important decisions turn on the answer we give to the former question.) Moreover, an anti-realist who sets out to investigate whether there is a fire out there is as likely to conclude that there *is* a fire out there as a realist, and will do so on exactly the same evidence. The conflicting philosophical viewpoints are therefore substantively and procedurally irrelevant. They have no bearing on whether the building is on fire, and no bearing either on how we should seek to establish whether the building is on fire. In the same way, it is not clear that conflicting philosophical viewpoints on metaphysical issues have any substantive or procedural implications for classicists engaged in interpreting classical texts.

But this, though it helps to illustrate my claim that philosophical debates will often have a limited bearing on practice, hardly does justice to Fowler's point. What classical scholars are, on his account, determined to situate 'out there' is *their stories*. To see whether that detail is important, let us go back to the interrupted philosophy seminar. In response to the student's question 'Is there a fire "out there"?', the tutor opens the door, sees billowing smoke and exclaims, 'There *is* a fire out there!' The student retorts: 'But when you say that there is a fire out there, is the story you are telling "out there"?' This question is even more puzzling than the preceding one: it is quite unclear what it would mean to answer either 'yes' or 'no'. To make sense of this question, therefore, we will have to examine the alternative which Fowler offers to stories being 'out there', and the objection which he brings against it.

Situating my stories 'out there' involves 'pretending that I didn't *make it all up*'. Of course, the point is not *my* making them up (as distinct from my learning them from a teacher or inheriting them from a tradition). Rather, being 'out there' is opposed to having been made up by anyone at all. So did the tutor make up the claim that there *is* a fire out there? Yes. The tutor's claim is based on a process of observation and inference, and in that sense at least it is undeniably constructed. And at a deeper level, the conceptual and linguistic resources needed to make the claim are social constructs. Does that tell us anything interesting about it? Within a philosophical frame of reference, perhaps: it is conceivably relevant to issues in epistemology. In a practical frame of reference, no: recognising the constructed nature of the tutor's claim does not tell us, for example, whether it is true or false (that is, whether there is or is not a fire out there); it does not tell us how we might try to establish its truth or falsity; and it gives us no help at all in deciding what we should do in response to the claim. Again, we seem to have reached substantive and procedural irrelevance.

Let us turn, then, to the problem that Fowler detects when classical scholars do 'situate their stories "out there" ': 'even the most apparently objective features of their texts are up for grabs.' Again, the formulation is not completely clear. If it means that there is scope for disagreement about features of the texts, it simply returns us to this chapter's starting-point. Sometimes disagreement stems from the inadequacy of our evidence. For example, the question 'Where did we go for dinner last time you were here?' may provoke disagreement if Delia and Eric have different recollections of where they went. There is some restaurant of which it would be true to say that they went there, but in the absence of evidence it may be impossible to reach agreement about which restaurant it was. Not all questions work like this. If Delia asks 'Where are we going to have dinner tonight?', what is required is not a statement of fact but a decision; there is no right answer until the decision has been made – shall we say, until the decision has been made there is no answer 'out there'? Perhaps, then, this has brought us to Fowler's real point: the questions that classical scholars concern themselves with require decisions, not statements of fact, and there are therefore no right answers (not even unknown ones) antecedent to our decisions.

A philosophical argument to the effect that every question was of the kind that demanded a decision as its answer rather than a statement of fact would be an important exception to my claim that philosophical positions often have a limited bearing on practice. There is no denying that such an argument would make a radical difference in practice, if its conclusions were accepted. If its conclusions are not accepted, however, the argument will be radically void of practical consequence. And it is difficult to see what kind of argument could warrant accepting such conclusions. Even if we restrict ourselves to questions of concern to classical scholars, the generalisation is wholly implausible. Consider, for example, the treatise *On Sublimity* traditionally attributed to Longinus. I have argued that it was, after all, written by Longinus, and dates to the third century CE.[4] But I do not think that this is certain; and though I hope my arguments will dent the modern consensus that the contents of the text are inconsistent with a third-century date, and that it therefore cannot have been written by Longinus, I do not expect to win over the whole scholarly community to a new consensus. The date and authorship of this text are indeed 'up for grabs', in the sense that any answer we give is open to debate and is likely to remain so. But our inability to establish conclusively who wrote this text and when it was written is evidence only of the limitations of our knowledge. It does not mean that the text was not written by anyone in particular over any particular period of time. The fact that we do not know, and have no way to achieve a consensus about, the right answer to a question does not imply that the question has no answer.

It might still be felt that if any answer we give is a story that we have made up, the question does not *really* have an answer. This feeling is shared (I suspect) by those who fear that the interpretation of classical literature is being sold out to subjective fantasies, and by those who celebrate its liberation from positivist dogma. But this is an illusion, arising from a failure to adjust fully to a change of idiom. In the old idiom stories were distinguished from knowledge of the real world. Now we are using 'story' to express the insight that human knowledge is constructed – an artefact that we create through processes of (among other things) observation and enquiry. In this new idiom, *every* factual claim we make is a story. (We do not

27

create the world, but of course we create our ways of describing the world.) Once we have stretched the term 'story' this far, we must let go of the dismissive connotations that the word acquired from its old contrastive use. All human knowledge is *telling stories*: conversely, then, telling stories is how human beings *know*. We have no grounds for drawing conclusions about the status or warrant of any particular claim simply from the fact that it is (in our new usage) a story, since there is nothing (in this usage) that is not a story. Accepting that our interpretations of classical literature are stories that we have made up no longer distinguishes those interpretations from anything else.

But surely (it might be objected) our stories have to be based on something – we can't *just* make them up. For example, my story about the authorship and date of *On Sublimity* is based on a number of different kinds of evidence, such as evidence for Longinus' literary critical interests and for the chronological distribution of the treatise's vocabulary. But that is just another way of saying that it is based on other stories that I want to tell. Our knowledge is stories all the way down – or (shifting the axis of the metaphor) our knowledge is a web of mutually supporting stories (beliefs, theories, hypotheses, conjectures ...), rather than an edifice raised on a fixed foundation. (Recall what we said in an earlier section (§1.2) about networks of interrelated propositions.) The 'web of belief' is a classic image of the anti-foundationalist analysis of knowledge, and what I have just said amounts to a declaration of philosophical allegiance. Philosophers who take a different approach to the analysis of knowledge would doubtless wish to raise objections at this point. Predictably, however, that philosophical debate will have no substantive or procedural significance for the interpretation of classical texts. It cannot: no one could ever seriously propose as candidates for foundational knowledge propositions of the kind that classicists put forward as interpretations, or as evidence in support of their interpretations. One might want to argue that (say) what is immediately given in sensory experience is foundational to human knowing (I wouldn't); but no one would dream of making a similar case for propositions about (say) the distribution of the term *stomphos* in extant Greek literary criticism, or the structure of Athenian civic ideology.

At this point I must confess that I have again been misrepresenting Fowler to suit my own expository convenience. For his primary concern in the essay from which I have quoted is not with philosophical questions as such. His suggestion is rather that classical scholars might learn how to respond to developments within their own discipline by observing the response that analogous developments have elicited within philosophy (p. 7):

> Irony has become central to postmodern attempts to cope with the abandonment of 'foundationalism'. I want to suggest that these attempts may help to alleviate some of the resistance to theory in a classical community which has similarly to face the loss of its foundations.

When in due course Fowler invokes Richard Rorty (p. 31), it is not primarily to commend a specific philosophical position. The suggestion is rather that the way in which Rorty reconciles his anti-foundationalist philosophy with moral and political commitment through the adoption of an ironist stance may provide classicists troubled by the loss of foundations with a model of how to cope. For the reasons already given, I do not think that the abandonment of foundationalism within philosophy is the kind of thing that *needs* to be coped with. It does not pose a practical problem of any kind (except, perhaps, to a philosopher who has too incautiously staked his reputation on a foundationalist analysis of knowledge-claims). But it could still be that there is a problem about a loss of foundations in classical studies, and that we could beneficially apply to this genuine problem a response made elsewhere to an illusory one.

For that to be true, we would, of course, need to be able to give an account of the problem that classicists have to cope with that disentangles it from the illusory worries associated with philosophical anti-foundationalism. I am not sure that Fowler has succeeded in doing this. Unpacking his comment on the 'loss of foundations', Fowler writes (p. 7): 'If we are not trying to *discover* what Vergil meant or why the Peloponnesian War broke out: if we are only telling stories about the past: why bother?' This remains entangled in the illusion that philosophical anti-foundationalism poses a problem; for reasons explained above, I think the opposition between discovery and 'only' telling stories is bogus. Admittedly, this is put forward as a report of what 'many classical scholars' feel, not something that Fowler is necessarily endorsing himself. But he does commit himself to a similar dichotomy elsewhere ('meaning is constructed, not discovered'),[5] and he does not provide any other account of the 'loss of foundations'. So we shall have to run our own check to see whether the foundations of classical studies have gone missing.

1.5. Agreement

A first glance at the series of section headings in this chapter may have suggested a narrative of progress: from the confused disagreements of interpretative practice we ascend through reflection, theory and philosophy towards a lucid consensus, each step doing more to help disclose and resolve the misunderstandings that initially bogged us down. That, as you will by now have realised, was a hoax. Understanding classical literature is a complex, and will always therefore be a contentious, business. The appeal to theory and philosophy enlarges and enriches the field over which we contend; that is where its value lies, and not in any capacity to put an end to contention.

But the emphasis that I have placed on disagreement should not lead us into exaggeration. The persistence of disagreement does not mean that it is impossible to reach any agreement all. There is no reason to expect *overall* consensus; but experience suggests that discussion does modify positions, and that new consensuses can be established. Moreover, even disagreement presupposes some underlying agreement. For example, Alan and Barbara (§1.2) could not have disagreed about *Antigone* unless they had a lot of beliefs about the play in common. Most of those beliefs were so basic that they did not need to make them explicit to each other, or even to themselves. It can, in fact, be hard to see just how many shared beliefs are assumed in any interpretative discussion. The disputed points to which we explicitly direct our attention (the things we attend *to*) inevitably have more salience for us than the assumptions that we take tacitly for granted (the things we attend *from*). To get a sense of what things might be like if this background of shared beliefs were unavailable, let us imagine a genuinely alien interpreter. According to Zog (who is a Martian), *Antigone* is not concerned with Creon's edict about the burial of Polynices, nor, indeed, is there any character called Creon in the play; the opening words mean 'pickled cabbage is very cheap today'; and the assumption that the text is written in Greek is arbitrary and unfruitful. (When I first saw posters advertising the film *Die Kinder*, an arbitrary and unfruitful initial assumption about the language of the title led me into a dead-end of speculation concerning the film's parodic relation to *Die Hard*.) Moreover, Zog appears not to be producing these startling claims at random, as we might instinctively suppose; our challenges elicit elaborate and apparently systematic, though deeply baffling, attempts to explain and justify them. How could we even begin to engage in fruitful discussion about *Antigone* with someone who thinks like that? Could we, indeed, conduct any sensible discussion with someone who thinks like that? In principle, perhaps: we could not communicate with Zog at all if we did not have *some* shared beliefs, and they will provide us with a point of potential engagement. But by the time we have brought the discussion to that contact-point, we would long have ceased to be talking about the interpretation of *Antigone*.

Zog's beliefs about *Antigone* place him outside the range of contributors to scholarly debate on the interpretation of classical texts. From that perspective, if Zog is not a Martian, he is a nutter, and in either case he can safely be ignored. As interpreters of classical texts, we do not have to show why Zog's interpretations are wrong before we get down to the things that we want to discuss among ourselves; we already know that they are irrelevant. Of course, dear reader, you are free to say that you cannot see why Zog's views should be dismissed in such a high-handed way. But if you do say this, I will not believe you – I will assume that these are purely artificial doubts (philosophical doubts, like those that Descartes tried to disarm). And if you insist that you *really* think Zog's views deserve to be taken seriously, it will follow from what I have already said that you too are a nutter who can safely be ignored.

Is that a satisfactory response? Suppose Zog were to add: '... and Homer was a Roman.' That, too, would be crazy. But the claim that Homer was a Roman was probably not crazy in the first century BC, when a Greek literary scholar, Aristodemus of Nysa, advanced it.[6] Admittedly, it is likely that even then it was on the edge of acceptable scholarly discussion (so far as we can tell, the idea did not catch on); but that is not enough to make it crazy. In the 1980s the idea that epinician songs were composed for solo rather than choral performance was on the edge of acceptable scholarly discussion. My own initial reaction when Mary Lefkowitz explained her theory to me was one of profound, though I hope politely dissimulated, incredulity; but that was not enough to make it crazy. At least, I would like to think it wasn't, since I subsequently came round to the view that the theory may be right.[7] The crucial difference between Zog on the one hand and Aristodemus, Lefkowitz and myself on the other is that we were able to give arguments in favour of our theories that made sense against a background of assumptions which we shared with our scholarly peers. Even if others did not see those arguments as sufficient or compelling reasons for adopting the theories in question, they could recognise them as intelligible and reasonable contributions to the discussion.

This response might still be thought unsatisfactory. Those background assumptions are not immutable truths. The set of background assumptions that Aristodemus exploited to argue for a Roman Homer is no longer available to us for use in framing theories – except, of course, for theories about Aristodemus and his cultural context; but we cannot use his background assumptions for framing theories about *Homer*. Indeed, the fact that propositions gain significance from their relations with other propositions in a network (§1.2) means that Aristodemus' theory itself is in one sense no longer available to us. We can understand it, but we could not intelligibly assert it without massive reconstruction of other beliefs that we hold: if *we* said that Homer was a Roman, we would be saying something very different, and utterly absurd. Likewise, the set of background assumptions now shared within the scholarly community will not remain available forever. Indeed, if they have their intended effect challenges to received opinion on such issues as the performance of epinician or the authorship and date of *On Sublimity* will contribute to the transformation of the scholarly community's shared background assumptions.

The implication of this line of argument would be that the shared assumptions on which we base our interpretative discussions are undermined by their acknowledged contingency and mutability; if so, then we can no longer appeal to them in good faith to justify our interpretations, knowing as we do that we may end up abandoning them. This argument is profoundly misconceived. It is reasonable for me to base the activities I undertake today on what I believe today. What alternative is there? I have to base them on something, and it would be absurd to base them on things I *don't* believe. Of course, tomorrow I might stop believing many of the things I believe today; but that is no reason for not believing them today (after all, I do not expect to become infallible tomorrow, so tomorrow's change of mind might be mistaken too). The activities I undertake today include cognitive activities like drawing inferences or justifying interpretations. So anyone who wants to persuade me that I should not use my current beliefs in these cognitive contexts has got to give me a reason for disbelief. The fact that I may change my mind is not in itself sufficient reason for changing my mind: I need to be given *specific* reasons for modifying my current set of beliefs, arguments that will counter the specific reasons that I can give for holding them. If this challenge is taken up, the result will be a process that is cooperative in two respects. First, an interpreter who takes a self-critical stance is already committed to subjecting his beliefs to critical testing; the other person who takes up the challenge is sharing that burden, and may be able to make the testing process more rigorous by contributing arguments from her different perspective. Secondly, the other person can only do this if she starts from a set of assumptions at least partially shared with me, since we cannot even disagree productively unless we share some common ground.

Any interpretation is an inference based on background assumptions that in part will be disputed, but must in large part be agreed by the other interpreters with whom I wish to enter into dialogue. The element of consensus is necessary: discussion would otherwise be impossible. But as we noted earlier (§1.1), any consensus is likely to be in part a consensus in error. So consensus as such is not a goal, and an inability to achieve consensus (whether on an interpretation or on its disputed premises) is not sufficient reason for me to conclude that I am wrong. It *is* good reason for me to conclude that I *may* be wrong, and to proceed with caution. By this, I do not mean that we should necessarily adopt a cautious expository style, constantly hedging statements with markers of uncertainty. (If we take uncertainty for granted, what would be the point?) Rather, our underlying cognitive strategy, our approach to enquiry, should acknowledge our fallibility: it should be open to criticism and revision – both internal self-criticism and criticism arising from public discussion. Even so, while the arguments continue to convince me, I can reasonably continue to accept the conclusion they point to. In fact, it would be irrational *not* to accept the conclusion of apparently convincing arguments. The same holds true at the communal level. We are *entitled* to take as the basis for enquiry whatever we currently agree on, and to endorse the conclusions that such agreement leads to. But we are also *obliged* to recognise the likelihood that we are partially mistaken in our agreements, and hence to adopt a collectively critical and self-critical stance towards our current knowledge.

Agreement is therefore simultaneously something indispensable, and something that should make us wary. Consensus is the enabling condition of the process of enquiry, just as dissent is its dynamic. The outcome of fruitful enquiry is a transformation of the prior consensus. But a newly emergent consensus should not be regarded as secure territory from which further forays into a shrinking unknown can be launched. The new consensus may simply express a shared bias or blind spot of the current community of interpreters. What self-critical enquiry achieves is always another provisional starting-point for further self-critical enquiry.

We can now return to the loss of foundations that we need, on Fowler's view, to cope with. If that means the loss of an extensive common ground which classicists can take for granted among themselves, it is now clear how serious a crisis would result from such a loss. It would put an end to any possibility of intelligent and intelligible discussion. But for that very reason I do not believe it can plausibly be maintained that such a crisis is upon us. Certainly, Fowler's own practice provides no evidence of it. His stories about classical literature are easy to tell apart from Zog's. They prove that substantial foundations are still in place – or, as we anti-foundationalists would prefer to say, that we still have access to an extensive network of beliefs shared with our disciplinary peers. No doubt we sometimes feel, less optimistically, that there has been an erosion of shared certainties amounting to a critical loss of foundations. It may well be that we disagree on more things than we used to. But the salience of the areas of explicit dispute should not distract us from the far more extensive field of things that are tacitly assumed in common. It may also be that, as the area of disagreement has expanded, we have become more aware of how intractable our disagreements are. But why should that alarm us? An awareness of the complexities and uncertainties of the material with which we are dealing is evidence that the process of critical enquiry is functioning as it should. That, surely, is not a problem to be coped with, but an achievement to be acclaimed.

2

Variety in interpretation

There are many ways to interpret a classical text. As we have seen, different interpreters give different answers to the same question; they ask different questions; and they disagree about which questions *should* be asked. In this chapter we shall explore some implications of the pluralistic context in which we inevitably operate as interpreters of classical texts.

2.1. Pluralism

What has been described is a context that is pluralist *de facto*. It does not follow that pluralism should be accepted (so to speak) *de jure*. The existence of multiple, competing and in at least some instances contradictory interpretative projects is inescapable, but it might be seen as a regrettable necessity. Alternatively, we might embrace this pluralism in principle as something to be valued.

The *de facto* pluralism would clearly be regrettable if it precluded fruitful dialogue at the level of interpretative practice. If, when two interpreters found themselves pursuing different interpretative projects, their only options were to ignore each other or to shift their exchange of views to a theoretical level, this would represent an impoverishment of our discussion. But the experience of Alan and Barbara (§1.2) suggests that this is not (or not necessarily) the case. Alan's enquiry into Sophocles' intentions and Barbara's enquiry into the contemporary reception of *Antigone* worked from an evidential base that was shared to a very large extent; much of what each of them said was therefore potentially relevant to the other's enquiry, and a fruitful exchange of ideas ensued. Let us assume that Charles (who objected to Alan's intentionalism) thinks that the interpreter's business is to establish the inherent meaning of the text itself. This is a project which Alan regards as profoundly muddled (the theoretical dispute between them is two-way). Even so, as they develop their respective interpretations they are both likely to pick out certain features of the text and explore their connections with other features. So it is perfectly possible that they will learn from each other's interpretations, despite a disagreement at the theoretical level which makes it impossible for either to accept the other's interpretation as a whole or in its own terms. Moreover, interpretative practice is rooted in the tacit skills that are acquired through ordinary social intercourse (§1.3). Even where, for the purposes of scholarly enquiry, we have become reflective interpreters, our practice is likely to be underdetermined by our theory. The continuing influence of pre-reflective interpretative skill means that interpreters who ask, or conceive themselves as asking, different questions may nevertheless have much in common in their practice.

The possibility of fruitful co-existence, though reassuring, does not resolve the issue of principle. Perhaps we should be striving to eliminate pluralism by determining, through theoretical reflection, which question (or questions) we should *really* be asking. On this view the evaluative level of reflection would be restrictive in aspiration, at least: its task would be to seek a *correct* theory of interpretation that will establish the pre-eminent validity of one interpretative question (or set of questions). Of course, this would require us to establish a theoretical consensus that we are not in fact likely ever to achieve; but feasibility in practice and desirability in principle are separate issues. Even in principle, however, there is compelling reason to deny that this restrictive aspiration is desirable. I have argued (§1.1) that a stable consensus at the level of interpretative practice would expose us to the risk of being immobilised in error; disagreement has a positive function in motivating enquiry. Analogously, a stable consensus about appropriate interpretative projects would make it possible for us all to be going in the same wrong direction. If we are all in the same boat, we may all sink together.

This is not to say that we cannot or should not subject interpretative questions to theoretical critique. I can see no advantage in a *general* aspiration to eliminate pluralism. But if a *particular* interpretative project seems to be incoherent, to rest on false assumptions, or to be in some other way defective, then it is perfectly appropriate to criticise it – and potentially beneficial: disagreement, I have argued, has a productive value as the dynamic of enquiry. So anyone who believes that intentions are intrinsically unknowable has good reason to criticise the project of intentionalist interpreters, and I as an intentionalist have good reason to listen to and consider their critique. On the other hand, talk about the play of signifiers will not impress anyone who thinks that the apparatus of signified and signifier expresses a basically flawed way of thinking about language. And an atheist invited to determine what God is saying to today's Church through a particular biblical passage will reasonably object that this is a project that in principle cannot be realised.

At this point, I want to return to the theoretical dispute between Alan and Charles; this illustrative detour will in due course lead us back to the necessity of pluralism. Alan believes that Charles' project of establishing the inherent meaning of the text itself is incoherent and impossible. It is therefore justifiable for him to raise objections to it. For example, what is the inherent meaning of the sentence 'I like cats for breakfast'?[1] We can analyse its linguistic structure – its syntax and lexicon; but that does not take us very far. Part of the problem, of course, is that we are being asked to interpret the sentence without a context. If we supply a context, perhaps the rules governing higher-level linguistic structures and the principles of pragmatics will generate a richer interpretation. Consider the following dialogue:

Man: I hope Mabel sleeps late again this morning. I can't cope with her sharp tongue this early in the morning.
Wife: Well, she's your sister.
Daughter: I like cats for breakfast.

At first sight we might be tempted to say that the sentence can now be seen as inherently meaningful in context. It means something like: 'I find people who make malicious comments entertaining company at breakfast, so I would be perfectly happy if Aunt Mabel joined us.' In fact, however, the relevance of the context is mediated through the subjective perspectives of the participants. For example, we would not be able to attribute this context-sensitive meaning to the sentence if we knew that the daughter had obsessively repeated that sentence and no other since her accident five years ago. Or suppose that the family's pet cat has just entered the room. Is the daughter drawing attention to the cat instead of referring to the aunt (perhaps in an attempt to head off her parents' imminent quarrel)? Or is her remark deliberately ambiguous? But if she had her back to the door, and could not have seen the cat, we could not interpret her utterance as drawing attention to it. So it is not the objective context that leads us to an utterance's contextual meaning, but the context as mediated through the speaker's individual point of view – or (more precisely) through the interpreter's perception of the speaker's point of view. Hence it is not only the participants' perspectives, but also their meta-perspectives (their perspectives on each others' perspectives), that mediate contextual meaning. Context is constructed intersubjectively.

It is certainly true that there are things that could be said about the daughter's utterance that are not in any way dependent on what she saw and meant. As has already been acknowledged, there are legitimate questions that restrict themselves to a purely linguistic analysis; however, interpretation would be deeply impoverished if we were limited to them. More interestingly, someone who had seen the cat entering the room might register a *potential* for ambiguity in context, despite being aware that the speaker was not in a position to exploit it deliberately. Likewise, we who posit the situation are able to register that potential. This suggests that meaning is to be understood, not as something inherent in the text itself, but as the meaning that someone (an utterer or hearer or reader) gives or might give to the text.

This argument does not, of course, lead to intentionalism as it is conventionally understood: first because it recognises hearers and readers as sources of meaning, as well as speakers and writers; secondly because in saying 'gives *or might give*' we open up the field to hypothetical or counterfactual speakers and writers. So we are not committed to seeing interpretation as an enquiry into the actual intention of an actual author. One can also ask, for example, what someone *might* have meant by this, or what someone *would* probably have meant by this (in specified circumstances). The point of the argument, therefore, is not to assert any particular interpretative project, but to expose the incoherence of any project that depends on the concept of meaning as something inherent in texts. I myself find this line of argument convincing; others, no doubt, will not. Theories (I am using the term here not in the sense of reflection on interpretative practices, as in §1.3, but in the sense of propositions at a relatively high level of abstraction regarding some concept or subject-matter) are as much a locus of disagreement as anything else. So we should be as wary of theories as of philosophies. We should not assume that having a theory of meaning (or language, textuality, society, ideology, gender …) will enable us to subordinate interpretative practice to a superior wisdom.

This point puts an obstacle in the path of one possible anti-pluralist strategy. Interpretation, it could be argued, is concerned with meaning. 'What does this mean?' is the question that epitomises the interpreter's task. So if we can figure out what meaning really is (if we can get a good theory of meaning), we will know what it is that interpreters should really concern themselves with. In my view, however, we would be ill-advised to treat any theory so incautiously. But this anti-pluralist strategy is hopeless for another, more pro-found reason. 'What does this mean?' is a pseudo-question. It does not tell us what we need to know about what is actually being asked. In particular, I will have little idea how to go about answering it unless I can frame (explicitly or implicitly) more specific questions to pose. It is those specific questions that give the question of meaning its meaning. In the same way, labelling something 'a reading' or 'an interpretation' does not tell us, even in very general terms, what question it is answer-ing. These are just umbrella words covering an indefinitely wide range of things one can do with texts. Moreover, even if someone thought that 'meaning' did have an intrinsic mean-ing, no consequence would follow, since no one is under an obligation to ask the question 'What does this mean?' at all. It is open to us to say: 'If interpretation means asking "What does this mean?" *in that sense*, then I am not an interpreter. But so what? Why should I be an interpreter *in that sense*?' An anti-pluralist strategy based on a theory of meaning would therefore end up in a stultifying argument about what labels we should attach to each other.

I can do with texts whatever I choose to do. If I choose to ask what encoding system would map *Antigone* onto the Leeds area telephone directory, I am free to do so. Of course, I will not. My choices are not arbitrary, and that would be an utterly pointless and uninteresting question. (It is also true that asking it would not advance my career. But even as a professional classicist, I ask questions primarily because they interest me.)

Hence the evaluation of interpretative questions does not depend solely on theoretical considerations (for example, whether the questions are coherent and well-founded), but also on our interests and purposes. This means that the question 'How should I interpret a classical text?' (in the sense, what interpretative questions should I be asking) *cannot* have a single answer. The correctness, aptness or interest of an interpretative project is necessarily relative to, and can only be determined in the light of, the end or ends to which we are reading; and those ends are in fact many and diverse. Interpretation enters into many different projects, in many different ways. Pluralism is therefore ineliminable in principle as well as in practice.

2.2. Questions

Affirming pluralism in principle and in practice does not remove the obligation to *clarify* our questions. If anything, it adds urgency to the need to avoid talking at cross-purposes. Clarification is also important because questions do not necessarily reveal their underlying structure openly. The question 'Where are we going to have dinner tonight?' might be the opening move in an attempt to reach a decision (which is the way we interpreted it in §1.4), or it might be a request for factual information about the arrangements that have already been made for tonight's dinner. The same observations might function in different ways in answers to the two questions. For example, 'Fiona hates seafood' might be offered as a reason for excluding seafood restaurants from the decision, or as a reason for thinking that George won't have booked a table at a seafood restaurant. To understand the arguments advanced in any interpretative discussion, therefore, it is important to be clear about the kind of questions that are being asked and answered.

We also – still – have an obligation to *evaluate* our questions. But in the light of the preceding section we can now identify two levels of evaluation. We need to ask whether the question is coherent, based on reasonable assumptions, and so on; but we also need to ask whether it is an interesting question, one worth asking. In Chapter 3, I shall try to clarify and evaluate questions about authorial intention; but first, in the rest of this chapter, I wish to give further thought to the relativity of interpretative questions to the interpreter's interests.

Let us suppose that an unusually imaginative aunt gives me a strange object as a present for Christmas. I might be moved to wonder: what on earth is the point of it? If so, there are various things that I might be wondering. First, what is it? What is it for? What could have possessed anyone to produce such a thing? Secondly, even if I recognise it as an ornamental Ruritanian doodah, I might still wonder: what can I do with one of those? So here are two conceptually distinct kinds of question about the object. The first addresses its purposiveness: what was it designed for, what was it made for? The second attempts to relate the object to my own interests and concerns: what can I do with it?

But the distinction between these two kinds of question is not a symmetrical one. I can ask the second kind of question (the one which tries to relate the object to my own interests and concerns) without worrying about the object's purposiveness. I may be so delighted to have something which meets my need for a paperweight that it never occurs to me to wonder what function it was originally designed to fulfil. Its original function may be completely irrelevant to my interest in and use for the object. But the converse does not hold. I cannot ask the first question (what was this designed or made for?) without relating the object to my own interests and concerns. For if I am asking this question, then (by definition) one of the interests or concerns that I have is to know what the thing was designed or made for. Compare a third question: I might wonder why the aunt gave it to me. This question, like that concerning the object's design, addresses someone else's purposes. But asking it also necessarily relates to a purpose of my own (perhaps, with the aunt hovering for my reaction, I want to be able to frame a tactful expression of thanks, or perhaps I am just curious to know what she was thinking of). All the questions I might ask about the object arise out of, and seek to relate it in some way to, an interest or concern of my own.

Why might my interests include knowing what the thing was made for? There are many possible reasons. Perhaps it has been incorporated into a guessing-game, with a prize if I get the right answer. Perhaps I have decided to sell it, and need to know what kind of person might buy it. That is to say, I may have ulterior purposes – purposes (like winning a prize or engaging in profitable trade) which have no intrinsic relation to knowing the purpose of this object, but which as it happens I cannot achieve unless I know what the object's purpose is. But that is not necessarily so. It may simply be that the object itself has stimulated my curiosity. In this case, getting an answer to my question about the purpose of the object will satisfy my curiosity; and there need not be any ulterior purpose in my enquiry beyond that. It seems to me quite plausible that I should be exercised by such curiosity. I am, after all, human, and 'all human beings by nature desire knowledge' – or so Aristotle tells us (*Metaphysics* 980a21). It is, in his view (and in mine), part of the natural structure of being human that things excite our wonder, and prompt us to ask questions.

2.3. Questions of interpretation

Imagine a congregation singing Cardinal Newman's hymn 'Firmly I believe and truly'. One member of the congregation (let us call her Helen), more strongly Protestant in her theological leanings than the rest, contemplates the imminent approach of the verse about 'Holy Church' with a realisation that she could not sincerely sing those words ('And I hold in veneration / For the love of Him alone / Holy Church as His creation / and her teaching as His own') in the sense that Newman probably intended them. Her options, then, are insincerity, silence or an affirmation of the words in some other sense. If she takes the third option she might find herself asking (for example) 'What sense can these words carry that is consistent with my neo-Reformed understanding of the church?' Newman's intentions are irrelevant to her, and have no claim to authority. In fact, from the perspective of someone who has to ask *that* question, Newman's intentions would, if authoritative, render the hymn unavailable for liturgical use. The criteria by which we assess the appropriateness or inappropriateness of the meaning that someone gives to a text must depend on the nature of their engagement with that text. In the context of an act of worship, theological rather than historical criteria are relevant.

Helen might then go home and reflect that she is less clear than she supposed as to what exactly Newman did intend when he wrote the words she found liturgically problematic. She does not know, for example, whether he wrote the hymn before or after his conversion to Rome; and even if (as she suspects) it was after, she is rather vague about the details of the Roman Catholic doctrine of the church. And she feels that this lack of understanding of Catholic ecclesiology is a gap she ought to fill – not because she expects it to have to any bearing on her own belief or worship, but because she is researching a doctoral thesis on nineteenth-century ecclesiastical history. So Newman's intentions have now become relevant. Helen has decided that to answer the historical questions in relation to which she has now begun to consider the hymn she needs to construct a hypothesis about Newman's doctrine of the church at the time he wrote it, and to ask what sense the words of the hymn can carry in the light, not of her own doctrine of the church, but of her model of Newman's doctrine. Of course, there are other historical questions which would not depend on Newman's intentions. For example, if her research leads her to consider the reception of Newman's works by Anglicans, Helen may find that she does not need to think about what Newman meant by the hymn, but about the way in which others understood it. In this case, she will have to construct hypotheses about the ecclesiologies of the various individuals and groups who read or reacted to the hymn.

Whichever direction her historical research takes her, Helen's own religious beliefs are not relevant. That is to say, they are not relevant as evidence for establishing the correct interpretation of the hymn (correct, of course, in the context of whichever historical enquiry she is conducting, since it follows from what has been said that there is no universal criterion of correctness for interpretations). At another level, however, Helen's religious beliefs may be very important. Perhaps they provided her with the motive for embarking on research in ecclesiastical history in the first place. In that case, the meaning of Newman's words *within* the enquiry may derive from Newman's theology; but the fact that Newman's words had that meaning derives *its* meaning for Helen (its significance, shall we say?) indirectly from the interpreter's theology. By contrast, when she was singing the hymn Helen's theological beliefs were directly relevant.

The kind of interpretation that Helen was engaged in when singing the hymn is dogmatic – not in the sense 'closed-minded' (she is willing to engage in open-minded discussion about how best to reconcile the text with her theology, and is theologically open-minded as well), but in the more technical sense that it judges possible interpretations by the criterion of consistency with a doctrine that is already taken as given. Thus interpretation is here driven by the desired outcome: this is the kind of thing that we want the text to mean – how are we to get that result? In that respect it can be compared to interpretations by Biblical fundamentalists (whose overriding concern is to produce an interpretation consistent with the premise that the Bible is free from contradiction and inerrant), or poststructuralists (whose overriding concern is to produce an interpretation consistent with the premise that meaning is unstable, or that the text subverts the whole history of western metaphysics, or whatever).

Conservative critics of poststructuralist interpretation have sometimes complained that 'anything goes'. This is clearly not true: when did you last read a poststructuralist interpretation concluding that the text did, after all, unequivocally assert the possibility of stable meaning? The illusion of licence is created by the fact that a firm commitment to a predetermined outcome often leads to the application of exegetical strategies that seem to have no rationale *except* that they make the desired outcome possible. Hence the appearance of arbitrariness has tended to diminish as a repertoire of exegetical devices useful for achieving the desired ends has developed, becoming stable and more widely familiar – and in many cases adopted more widely within the larger community of interpreters.

The relativity of interpretation to interest means that neither fundamentalist nor poststructuralist interpretation is in principle wrong. But just as the former will be of limited interest to those who do not share its premise about divine inspiration, so demonstrations of the slippage of signifier and signified will be of limited interest to those who find this way of thinking about language unhelpful. I suggested earlier that these interpretative projects could be criticised as misconceived by those who do not share their premises; they may also be found simply *uninteresting* outside the circle of believers. This brings us back to the question of the possibility of fruitful dialogue in a context of *de facto* pluralism raised earlier (§2.1). Unless adherents of a particular interpretative project are willing to retreat into an insular clique, they have some reason to establish and maintain the kind of shared practices that make possible fruitful dialogue with those engaged in other projects. For example, some fundamentalists are content to address a community of like-minded religious believers, but a conservatively inclined academic specialist in biblical studies, even if he makes the same assumptions about inerrancy, has simultaneously to address a scholarly community that does not share that commitment. This imposes an additional constraint on how he goes about constructing an interpretation of the biblical text consistent with his own assumptions. His arguments have to fall within a range acceptable to his disciplinary peers. If this constraint is observed, his interpretations need not be seen as hopelessly compromised by his fundamentalist commitments; they can be evaluated by other scholars for the contribution they might make towards their own, differently conceived interpretative projects. Pluralism does not necessarily inhibit fruitful interchange, therefore; but we will certainly have to make an effort if we are to keep the possibility alive.

2.4. Meaning and significance

What will count as the meaning of a text depends on what questions we are asking (are we, for example, asking questions about the author's intentions?); which questions we ask will depend on the nature of our interest in the text. But statements about the text's meaning, however defined, are not the only kind of statement that we want to make. There are also descriptive statements (for example: this text is self-contradictory) and evaluative statements (which stand in a complex relation to descriptions: self-contradiction is likely to have different implications for the quality of a philosophical treatise and a nonsense poem). But how are we to decide what to say? Exhaustive description is impossible; and even if it were possible, it would not be desirable or useful. The fact that a statement is true is not enough to make it worth saying; many truths are trivial, arbitrary or irrelevant. We need to pre-empt the challenge 'So what?' So our selection of things to say about the text (whether they are statements about meaning, or descriptive or evaluative statements) will also be governed by the nature of our interest in the text. Another way of putting this would be that the selection of a criterion of meaning (what will *count* as a meaning within a particular interpretative project), and our selection of descriptive or evaluative statements about a text as interpreted in accordance with that criterion, are both determined by reference to the *significance* they bear in relation to some interest which an interpreter is taking in that text. Significance, therefore, is a more fundamental concept in the theory of interpretation than meaning. (We can now see from a different perspective why a theory of meaning cannot provide an anti-pluralist strategy (§2.1): if a statement about a text has significance, it is of interest to us whether or not what it tells us about is a 'meaning'; if it does not have significance it does not earn its place in an interpretation, even if it tells us about a 'meaning'.)

Some clarification may be necessary here. The word 'significance', which I introduced in the course of our discussion of Helen's research (§2.3), may seem straightforward, but it has been used in a variety of ways. In drawing the distinction between meaning and significance as I have just done I am making a point rather different from that which E.D. Hirsch made using the same pair of terms. He defines the two terms as follows:[2]

> In the present book 'meaning' refers to the whole verbal meaning of a text, and 'significance' to textual meaning in relation to a larger context .... In other words, 'significance' is textual meaning as related to some context, indeed any context, beyond itself.

In my account, by contrast, a text's relational properties have no particular privilege among its describable properties in general, and none of those properties are significant in themselves. Significance arises when any property of a text (including, but not only, those properties we might call 'meanings', and including relational properties – that is, properties that the text possesses in relation to some context) is brought into relation with an interpreter's interest in the text. Hence in the following passage Don Fowler has badly misunderstood my position. The context is a discussion of descriptive ekphrases in classical narrative. After confronting post-modernist critics who would claim that his desire to integrate such ekphrases interpretatively is totalising and authoritarian, Fowler continues:[3]

> Moreover, the modernist classical critic is likely to find herself stabbed in the back by reception theorists like Malcolm Heath, who would deny that ancient readers would have felt this *need to interpret* which is the standard starting-point for accounts of ekphrasis. I do not myself believe that Heath is right. Basic to his approach

is the Hirschian opposition between 'meaning' (identified with conscious intention) and wider 'significance'
as read in by modern interpreters, and the exaltation of
the former characterized as historical over the latter
characterized as 'the forceful imposition of alien preconceptions on ancient literature'.

This gets my approach wrong on three counts. First, I do not
identify meaning with *anything* in particular; 'meaning', in the
account that I have given, is a variable that gets its content
from whatever questions an interpreter happens to be asking
(§2.1). Secondly, in so far as I am interested in the meanings
which authors intended, I have no particular interest in 'conscious' intention (a point to which we shall return in §3.1).
Thirdly, as just noted, my use of the terms 'meaning' and
'significance' is not consistent with Hirsch's. And if you construe the distinction as I have done, it makes no sense at all to
'exalt' meaning over significance; for meaning does not exist
without significance. There is no point in asking what a text
means except in relation to some interest you have in that text.
Indeed, the very idea of doing so is incoherent, since what will
count as an answer to the question 'What does this mean?'
depends on the nature of your interest in the text. Significance
is the condition of the possibility of meaning.

The words which Fowler quotes at the end of this passage
do not distinguish meaning from significance; they are concerned, rather, with different kinds of meaning – that is, with
different interpretative questions. When I wrote them, I was
making a gesture (too brusque, no doubt, and too opaque)
towards the reasons why one kind of meaning has particular

significance for me – why, in other words, I find the kind of historically oriented questions I was asking in the book from which the quotation comes ('what did ancient authors mean, and how did ancient readers understand them?') more interesting than certain other questions. But the validity of other questions is something that I explicitly recognised in the same context:[4]

> To speak of texts being 'rightly' interpreted presupposes a normative standard of interpretation, a criterion of meaning; and no such criterion can lay claim to exclusive validity. The aptness of an answer depends on the questions asked ... I have offered no arguments against interpretations that make no claim to historical validity of that kind; in other contexts and for other purposes, I would not necessarily wish to reject them.

This chapter will, I hope, have done something to elucidate and explain the rationale of that statement of pluralistic principle. But there is clearly also more work to be done in explaining why I find the kinds of question I was asking in that book (and in other books and articles that I have written) interesting. That is one of the issues to be addressed in the next chapter.

3

Good intentions

Disagreement can be fruitful, but not every difference is a disagreement. Different answers to different questions do not necessarily conflict; different questions do not necessarily conflict, either, since there is an open-ended plurality of questions that can sensibly be asked. But this is not an argument for indiscriminate pluralism. Not every question can sensibly be asked; some questions are pointless, and some are misconceived. Here, therefore, the potential for disagreement re-emerges.

I am inescapably implicated in one such disagreement. There has been much debate in modern literary theory concerning the legitimacy and relevance of claims about authorial intention, and I have already indicated my willingness to make such claims. In this chapter I shall defend a version of intentionalism; in terms of the three levels of reflection identified in §1.3, I shall be offering a positive evaluation of questions about authorial intention. It is important to emphasise, however, that my defence presupposes the pluralist framework developed in the preceding chapter. So I shall argue that questions about authorial intention are worth asking, but I shall not argue that they are the only ones worth asking. On the contrary, it will become clear that anyone who wishes to ask intentionalist questions must ask other kinds of question as well (§3.1, (ix)-(xi)). Nor shall I argue that questions about authorial intention are necessary in any absolute sense. I shall argue instead that they are conditionally necessary – necessary if we wish to achieve certain purposes (§3.3). We may, if we wish, repudiate those purposes. But that will incur a cost, since the purposes include ones that classicists have typically had as classicists.

3.1. What are intentions?

Before I embark on the evaluation of intentionalist questions we need to do some preparatory work at the clarificatory level of reflection. Much anti-intentionalist argument has been based on seriously defective conceptions of intentionality. In this section I shall put forward a series of negative theses, in each case rebutting what I take to be a widespread misunderstanding of intention and intentionalism. The supporting commentary will sketch out the positive account that I wish to offer as an alternative. On this account, interpretative statements about authorial intention conceive of the author as an agent, and of the text as the product of an agent's purposive behaviour. This section is therefore an attempt to determine what is and what is not entailed by such a conception.

(i) *'Intention' should not be equated with 'conscious intention'.* This equation is a persistent reflex in anti-intentionalist writing. Its strength is shown, for example, by the quotation from Don Fowler discussed in §2.4, which attributes an identification of meaning with conscious intention to one intentionalist who states explicitly that 'there are usually components of an author's intended meaning that he is not conscious of',[1] and to another who has (so far as I can recall) *never* referred to *conscious* intention at all. In fact, I try to avoid reference to 'conscious' intention, because I have no clear idea what 'consciousness' is (philosophically it is a murky concept); nor, therefore, am I very sure in what sense or senses I believe in it. This means that I have no reliable way of telling what I am conscious of, let alone anyone else. But that is not a problem, since I do not regard the concept of consciousness as crucial to interpretation. What I am interested in is purposiveness: the composition of a text as a process directed towards some end or ends. Whether, and in what sense, the purposiveness is conscious may be of little consequence.

Consider, by way of illustration, an example of an action that is not textual. This morning I walked to the University – an intentional act. Was my intention *conscious*? The answer will depend on the nature of the implied contrast. Clearly the intention was not unconscious in a Freudian sense (it was not repressed). Nor was it unconscious in the sense used by some cognitive psychologists (describing levels of implicit processing that are in principle inaccessible to introspection). On the other hand, I was not attending reflexively to the intention of walking to the University while I did it. In fact, I was not even attending to the walking (I was so absorbed in planning a seminar that I scarcely noticed the journey). Nor did I have to form an explicit resolution to walk to the University before setting out (that is part of my daily routine, and I did it unreflectively). Yet in one sense I was aware of what I was doing (if anyone had asked me, I could have told them), and I was certainly doing it on purpose. So was there a conscious intention? The term is so vague that I am not sure how to answer. And I do not see what we would gain from having an answer. How would it advance our understanding of what I was doing?

I do not want to exaggerate this point. There is a vague, idiomatic use of 'conscious' that we can handle well enough, and there are times when it does make a difference whether we think that something was done with (in some sense of the word) conscious intent. An offensive remark knowingly intended as such will be judged differently, and evoke different responses, from one with offensive implications of which the utterer could not have been aware. But if the utterer could have been aware of the implications, it may also make a difference whether we judge his or her disclaimer of offensive intent to be wittingly deceitful or the product of unwitting self-deception. The very fact that we may, in some circumstances, want to differentiate cases such as these shows that the intentionalist's interest is not *limited* to conscious intention; and there is no reason to suppose that the question whether an intention was (in whatever sense) conscious will always be relevant.

(ii) *'Intention' should not be equated with a prior 'design or plan in the author's mind'*. This phrase, taken from Wimsatt and Beardsley's famous critique of the 'intentional fallacy',[2] overlooks a distinction between intentional action and an intention to act. The point can be explained by means of the illustration used in (i). When I left my house this morning I intended to walk to the University, and on this occasion what

3. Good intentions

I intended to do matched what I intentionally did. But sometimes there is a mismatch. On some mornings I intend to walk to the University, but in the event do not. For example, if I find that the pavements are very icy I might decide to take a bus instead. In that case, the intentional action actually undertaken diverges from the prior design or plan. This is not to deny that there are circumstances in which the prior design or plan might be interpretatively relevant. For example, someone observing my journey to the University on an icy day might find the unnecessarily circuitous route that I take to the bus stop puzzling. The explanation is that I started out in one direction with the intention of walking, but turned back towards the bus stop when I realised that the pavements were too hazardous. So what I ended up doing is intelligible only in the light of the prior plan that I abandoned. But this is because the abortive plan helps to make intelligible the complex intentional structure of what I actually did; the plan is not in itself an interpretation of what I did.

(iii) *To ask questions about the intentionality of an action is not to ask about the agent's psychological states as distinct from the action itself.* What is in view is the teleological structure of the action – its directedness towards some end or ends – and not some inner event or process separable from the performance of the action. So asking questions about authorial intention does not commit us to enquiring into the author's psyche *rather than* the text. The enquiry is precisely into the text as the product of purposive behaviour. The author is an indispensable element of the text conceived in this way, since the text *is* the product of purposive behaviour *because* it was produced by an author.

The kind of concern that I wish to counter here is apparent, for example, in the reason Oliver Lyne gives for surrendering the term 'allusion' in favour of 'intertext':[3]

> We have no evidence about Vergil's intentions in the matter of allusion *beyond the evidence of the text.* It is only texts we can reasonably talk about. Since the term 'allusion' encourages us to appeal to an entirely chimerical 'authorial intention' – to turn away from the text – it is best abandoned.

But what is at issue is not a choice between talking about the text and talking about something else; it is a matter of *how* one talks about the text – whether as the product of purposive activity or in some other way. The example which Lyne uses to lead into this reflection proves the point. Some interpreters, trying to understand the relationship between *Aeneid* 6.460 ('unwillingly, o queen, I departed from your shore', spoken by Aeneas to Dido in the underworld) and Catullus 66.39 ('unwillingly, o queen, I departed from your head', spoken by a constellation that was formerly a lock of Queen Berenice's hair), have found themselves unable to give a plausible account of the connection in terms of significant allusion, and have inferred that Virgil may therefore not have intended the allusion to be significant. To represent this as 'turning away from the text', Lyne has to describe the process in a peculiar way (p. 187):

3. Good intentions

We feel licensed to say that Vergil significantly alludes in *this* echo, but – if we cannot make sense of it – not in *that* one. And we retire contented. It will not do. We are making unjustifiable assumptions, we are forming pre-conceptions about an author's 'intentions' which we have no right or evidence to form.

Here a *conclusion* which some scholars have reached through reflecting on the text is reported as a *preconception* (why 'pre-', if not because forming conceptions would seem too innocuous a thing to do?); and the evidence from which the conclusion is inferred ('we cannot make sense of it') is no sooner reported than its existence is denied. I think it quite likely that the conclusion in question is wrong (the evidence offered is not *proof*: perhaps the required sense has simply been missed), but what is at issue here is not the factual correctness of the conclusion, but its methodological legiti-macy. It is perfectly reasonable to cite the difficulties that have been encountered in reading a text in a particular way (for example, as significantly allusive) as evidence that it was not intended to be read in that way. And it is precisely the *text* that is the object of attention when such an argument is put forward.

(iv) *Intentions are not necessarily transparent to the intender.* That such a lack of transparency is characteristic of agency in general follows from (among other things) the notion of tacit skills introduced in §1.4. The agnosticism about consciousness that I expressed in (i), which implies that reflexive awareness is not necessary to intention in the sense that I am using the term, reinforces the point.

Even where there is a reflexive awareness it may be mistaken. Interpreting myself is complexly different from interpreting others. It is true that I have access to more, and more kinds of, information with regard to myself than to others; I am aware of myself in ways that I cannot be aware of any other person. But self-awareness is not automatic (the observation (§1.5) that what we attend from has less salience than what we attend to is relevant here), and even the most basic level of self-awareness is not necessarily veridical (think, for example, of an amputee's phantom limb). Moreover, precisely because my self-awareness may give the appearance of being unproblematic I am likely to be less aware of its limitations as evidence; conversely, there are kinds of evidence that will be more salient to an observer than to me. Finally, of course, in one's own case the motives for misinterpretation are uniquely powerful: we are capable of self-deception (as was noted in (i)).

(v) *Authorial intention is not identical with an author's statements about the intention of a text.* This should be obvious: if authorial intention is not to be equated with an author's knowledge of his or her own intention, *a fortiori* it cannot be equated with an author's report of his or her own intention. Such a report may provide an interpreter with relevant evidence; it cannot, in itself, be decisive.

(vi) *Intention is not to be conceived as something stable and wholly determinate.* If I ask the fishmonger for a pound of squid, I will be dissatisfied if I am given an ounce or a ton; but I will not be happy either if the fishmonger, having weighed out 16½ ounces, spends the rest of the morning slicing off minute slivers of tentacle to achieve ever closer approximations to a pound. I am not asking for *exactly* a pound; but there is no specifiable range of outcomes that would satisfy my request either – trying to specify that range would lead to a form of the sorites paradox. (If you remove grains one by one from a heap of sand you will end up with something less than a heap, but there does not seem to be any point at which just one more grain will make the critical difference between what is and what is not a heap.) In fact, there is arguably no prior answer: offered 14 ounces, I do not inspect my intention to see if it stretches that far; I *decide* whether or not that is enough. Recall the distinction made in §1.4 between questions requiring a statement of fact and questions requiring a decision. In the present case we can distinguish between what is fact (I certainly do not want just one ounce) and what requires decision (will 14 ounces do?) – though the distinction itself is not clear-cut: there is a continuum with an indeterminate point of transition.

My request is therefore indeterminate. More precisely, it is not completely determinate. For it is not vacuously indeterminate. Given the teleological structure of each party's involvement in the transaction, it is possible to reach interactively a conclusion about what will count as satisfying my request that is by no means arbitrary. (Replace the fishmonger with a poststructuralist critic, whose purposes are different, and the indeterminacy of my request might begin to seem less tractable.) Indeterminacy therefore does not constitute a practical problem. On the contrary, indeterminacies in intention are crucial to practice, since organisms that could only formulate and act on highly determinate intentions would be unable to operate effectively in a complex, ever-changing and incompletely predictable environment; indeterminacy provides for the flexibility that such an environment requires. So my request to the fishmonger is not an isolated or exceptional instance. Indeterminacy is part of the normal structure of intentionality. Intentions typically have a penumbra of vagueness.

(vii) *Intentionalists are not committed to an exhaustive or wholly determinate grasp of authorial intentions.* It follows from the typical indeterminacy of intentions that such a commitment would be impossible to fulfil; indeterminate intentions can only be indeterminately known. But the commitment is in any case unnecessary, in the light of interpretation's relativity to interest (§2.4). I have argued that what will count as a meaning depends on what questions are being asked in a given interpretative enquiry, and that those questions in turn depend on the nature of the interest the interpreter has in the text. Likewise, what will count as an adequate answer to a given interpretative question depends entirely on the interpreter's interest. We do not in practice look for the best possible answer to a given question; we look for an answer that is *better* than the one we have already and *good enough* for the purposes we have in hand. (If this were not the case, we could never reach any conclusions.) Interpretation is always incomplete. The relativity of the criteria of correctness and adequacy in interpretation to the interpreter's interests explains why we need not be troubled by this fact.

(viii) *Intentionalists do not assume a single, univocal meaning.* An author intended whatever he or she intended (subject, as we saw in (vi), to a qualification about the typical indeterminacy of intentions). But that does not imply that the intended meaning must be either univocal (there are intended ambiguities) or single (consider utterances that have a subtext designed for those in the know). For example, there are at least two ways in which the utterance of 'I like cats for breakfast' in the context described in §2.1 might have been intendedly ambiguous (assuming the scenario in which the daughter had seen the pet cat enter the room). She might have intended an overt and stable ambiguity, establishing with the addressees a mutual awareness of the dual application of her remark; or she might have intended an elusive ambiguity, creating uncertainty on the part of the addressees as to whether any reference to the aunt was intended at all. And she might have intended both of these things simultaneously. For example, she might have wanted her father to be amused by his perception of the remark's intended ambiguity and her mother to be irritated by an unprovable suspicion of its malicious intent. (In that case the daughter might also have good reason not to acknowledge part of her intention, and we would have reason to distrust the reliability of anything she said about the innocence of her intent. She might not be honest even to herself with regard to the intention to annoy her mother. The example therefore also illustrates points made in (iv) and (v).)

In this example the ambiguity has a simple structure: the

daughter's utterance may be applied to either (or both) of two referents – Aunt Mabel and the cat. But this is not always the case; other ambiguities are more open-ended. Indeed, our observation on the indeterminacy of intentions (vi) indicates that a degree of pregnancy is typical of utterances. We often say things with the intention of eliciting a response within a range that has no precise intended limits. My request to the fishmonger provides a trivial example: I was asking for a pound of squid, or thereabouts. More interestingly, when I use an evocative metaphor it is unlikely that what I intend to convey has a clear, determinate limit. Perhaps there is a core of things that I definitely intend to convey, surrounded by a corona of progressively more remote associations. In addition, part of my intention may be to provide a stimulus to creative associations on the part of the audience that go beyond anything that I could have anticipated. In this case the intention's open-endedness is more radical.

(ix) *Intentionalists do not claim that intention is the only interesting feature of a text.* In the case of a metaphor intended to be radically open-ended (viii), we need to go beyond what is included in the intention in order to realise the metaphor's potential (that is what is intended!). But even an utterance that is intended to be unambiguous may nevertheless have an unintentional ambiguity. For example, we noted in the discussion of the daughter's utterance in §2.1 that an observer could legitimately register the potential dual application even if he realised that the daughter was not herself in a position to be aware of that potential.

Picking up the terminology of the opening paragraph of

3. Good intentions

§2.4, an intentionalist might say that in exploring the metaphor's evocative potential or in registering an unintentional ambiguity we provide a description of the text, rather than an interpretation of it (in the sense of a statement about its meaning or meanings). If we do adopt that terminology, however, it must be understood as a convenience for distinguishing meanings, in the limited sense that 'meaning' has within a given interpretative project, from other features of the text. Other interpretative projects will draw the distinction differently. And even within an intentionalist project, adopting or rejecting that terminological convention will have no consequences at all concerning the validity or value of a descriptive statement (for reasons explained in §2.1 and §2.4). Intentionalism does not imply that the description of unintended textual features is improper or irrelevant. Statements about intended meanings and statements about unintended features of a text (whether or not we choose to call them meanings) are not in competition with each other. There are purposes for which we may need both. For example, if we wish to advise someone to rephrase something he has written in order to avoid an obscene double meaning arising from a colloquialism of which he is not aware, we need to know *both* that there is an ambiguity *and* that it was unintended (if we thought that it was intended, we would give different advice).

(x) *Intentionalism does not imply that the author is viewed as an isolated individual.* Intentional activity is always embedded in a social context, and cannot be abstracted from that context. Consider the case of someone sitting in the chair at the head of the table and saying 'I declare this meeting open': he

71

intentionally opens the meeting. This is an intention that presupposes a complex of social institutions and norms. It cannot be formulated outside a social context, and can only be understood with reference to that social context.

Any action will have socially determined features that are not intention-dependent, and intentionalism does not require us to discard those features as irrelevant or uninteresting. As I have already emphasised (ix), an interest in intended meanings carries no implication that descriptive statements about textual features that are independent of intention are inherently uninteresting. What intentionalism does imply is that in understanding an action reference to intention cannot be wholly displaced in favour of its socially determined features. Consider again the case of someone who sits in the chair at the head of the table and says 'I declare this meeting open'. If we add that the person is not entitled to chair the meeting, this might be seen as a counterexample to an intentional theory of meaning; in this case (it might be argued) it is a social fact that determines the meaning of the act, not the intention. But it is not a counterexample to the kind of intentionalism that I have been outlining, which recognises the social context of intentional action, acknowledges that an action's intentionality is not its only interesting feature, and does not get hung up over the application of the word 'meaning'. In particular, this example does not provide any reason to deny the interpretative relevance of intention. Suppose that the speaker either (i) mistakenly believed that he was the chairman, or (ii) wittingly impersonated him. In the latter case, suppose that the impersonation was done (a) as a joke, or (b) as a hoax, or (c) as part of a fraud. The intentional structure of the action varies in these scenarios, and with it the account we would offer of the action – it would be positively misleading to describe a mistake and a fraud in the same terms. The example thus suggests that a concern with intention may be an ineliminable component of our dealings with texts, as well as an insufficient one. Indeed, the intentionality of the action may itself be the source of various institutional or social meanings: fraudulent intent is legally significant in a way that innocent confusion is not. Thus non-intentional meanings sometimes depend on the answers we give to questions about intention.

(xi) *Questions about intention cannot be the only questions an intentionalist asks.* On the contrary, if we are to form hypotheses about intention we have to ask questions about other things. In particular, since intentional action is always socially embedded (x), an understanding of the social context of the action has to be sought in parallel with an understanding of its intentionality.

(xii) *Explaining an action in terms of the agent's intentions does not preclude explanations in terms of deeper structures.* The intentionalist denies only that structural explanations provide a substitute for intentional explanation. From the intentionalist perspective, the author is the immediate producer of a text. If the author is, in turn, a product of (for example) language, society or ideology, then the text is also a product of these things. But that does not make reference to the author superfluous, since the production is mediated by the author. (My toaster was made in a factory, but that does not mean that I can elide the role of the toaster in giving an account of how this piece of bread became toast.) In the account I have been giving there is no deeply rooted antithesis between the individual and the social, since the individual is a socially constituted fact. But there is an important contrast between the particular and the general. The individual is a particular social fact, not a generalised one (in the way that concepts such as a language, a society or an ideology are generalisations); and the particularity of the text is the product of particularised, not solely of generalised, causes.

Consider, in this connection, Lowell Edmunds' description of the impact of Saussure:[4]

> With him came the notion of the arbitrariness of the linguistic sign, which is constituted within its system by its differential relation to other signs. Meaning thus belongs primarily to the system and is not a matter of the relation between the sign and something external to the system. With this notion, a revolution begins, because the user of language is no longer the autonomous subject exercising an intentional control over his linguistic creations. On the contrary, he is created by his language. The text likewise loses in autonomy and is seen to dissolve in the various larger systems – for example, intertextual ones, which enable it to have significance.

From the perspective that I have suggested, there are some questionable dichotomies in this passage. It is striking, for example, that meaning is 'primarily' systemic: the qualification implies that it is not exclusively systemic, and yet extra-systemic sources of meaning are seemingly excluded ('and

3. Good intentions

not') – how is this exclusion motivated? And why should a dependence on larger enabling systems be thought to 'dissolve' the text? More importantly, for my present purposes, what is the justification for the antithesis ('on the contrary') between the user of language exercising control and the user being created by language? Even within a Saussurean framework a distinction would need to be drawn between the language (system, *langue*) that creates the speaker and the language (utterance, *parole*) that is his or her creation. The creation of speakers by their language does not preclude speakers' exercise of intentional control over their utterances; on the contrary, it makes it possible. This is not, of course, to say that speakers can exercise *complete* control over their utterances: there are (as we noted in §2.1 and §3.1(ix)) facts about utterances that are independent of intention. But we did not need Saussure to tell us *that*.

The intentionalist is not committed, therefore, to denying the claim that the language user is created by his or her language. To what extent that claim is *right* is another question. Let us concede for the moment that the language I speak determines what I *can* say. It does not determine what I *do* say. People who speak the same language say different things. So language alone is not sufficient to explain the particularity of my linguistic behaviour; it cannot be language alone that creates me. The fact that I acquired a language in the first place confirms this. The acquisition of a first language is an extraordinarily complex business; so I existed, and possessed sophisticated cognitive capacities, before I had a language. This is not to deny that the acquisition of language profoundly changed me. It made my cognitive capacities more powerful,

75

and at the same time it imposed a certain contingent structure on those capacities (not all possibilities are equally accessible); the structure is a necessary condition of the enabling function. But one of the things that language enables me to do is to transcend the current state of my language. A language is never a complete and stable system (even though that is a convenient idealisation for linguists who are trying to describe a language from a synchronic point of view); it is always incomplete and open. That must be so, since a language cannot always have incorporated in advance the response to unpredictable new situations or kinds of situation. There is thus always potentially an improvisatory and creative element in our use (and, therefore, understanding) of language. So it is not even true that my language determines what I *can* say. Language transforms language users, who in turn transform their language. The relationship between language and language-users is not uni-directional ('the user of language ... is created by his language'), but dialectical.

Readers of an anti-humanist cast of mind might suspect at this point that some attempt is being made to smuggle in a notion of the wholly autonomous, self-creating individual genius. That is not the case. We may grant, if we wish, that the individual is completely determined by antecedent factors. Even if those factors were all structural, the complexity of the structures and of their interaction would mean that each individual is determined differently; so particular social facts (like authors) still could not be collapsed into a bundle of generalised social facts (language, society, ideology ...). But once we have granted that, it becomes obvious that the antecedent factors cannot all be structural. If particular social facts (such as people) cannot be reduced to generalities, nor can the influence they have on other particular social facts (such as other people). Human beings influence each other in complex and contingent ways that are dependent on, but cannot be reduced to, generalised structures. So, even granting the individual's complete determination by antecedent factors, the project of giving an account of social interactions and their products while eliding individuals and their intentions does not look promising.

*

I conclude this section with a cautionary example. Imagine an experiment in child psychology conducted along the following lines. An experimenter sets out two rows of counters, and asks a child whether there are more counters in one row than in another. The child answers (correctly) that there is the same number in both rows. The experimenter then spreads out the counters in one of the rows more widely and repeats the question. A series of tests of this kind was devised by Piaget, who found that a high proportion of children of a certain age would answer (incorrectly) that there were more counters in the row that had been spread out. At first sight this appears to reveal something interesting about children's reasoning and grasp of quantity. But subsequent researchers have found that a different result is obtained if the procedure is altered. If, for example, the experimenter leaves the room after spreading the counters out and someone else asks the repeat question, the proportion of children giving the correct answer increases significantly. Why? A plausible explanation is that the newcomer's question can be understood as a genuine request for information, so that the child feels no inhibition about repeating the answer given before. But when the question is put a second time by the same person it is not so easy to see it as a straightforward request for information (the child knows that the questioner has already been given the relevant information); so there is implicit encouragement to look for another interpretation of the question – perhaps as an invitation (backed up by adult authority) to reconsider and revise an unsatisfactory initial response.[5]

What the experiment actually reveals, therefore, is the children's sensitivity to the perspective of the other party in a dialogue. In this case, the flawed design of the original experiment thwarted the children's attempt to understand and respond appropriately to the other party's intentions. The experimenter's failure to consider the children's perspective, or to recognise that they were partners in a dialogue, made the establishment of intersubjectivity (§2.1) impossible. We, for our part, in trying to understand the interaction have to consider the intentions of both parties (our conjecture about what the children were trying to respond to is significant *because* we also realise that this is not what the experimenter really meant). But that is not to say that our understanding of the interaction as a whole can be reduced to propositions about the two parties' intentions. Rather, an understanding of their respective intentions opens the way to a richer descriptive grasp of what was happening between them. Thus the example confirms both that we are not limited to interpretation in terms of intention (see (ix)-(xi) above), and also that there is no short cut which by-passes intention.

3. Good intentions

3.2. Are intentions knowable?

The preceding section has not attempted to give a comprehensive account of intention; it is an outline sketch, designed to indicate why I believe that intentionalists are not committed to a position inherently flawed in the ways often suggested by anti-intentionalist polemic. But there is still an important issue to address: this defence of intentionalism will be fruitless if intentions are inherently inscrutable.

I have argued (§3.1(iii)) that intention is not a purely private, inward matter: it is part of the structure of the action, and – as such – potentially open to observation. That is not to say, however, that an action's overt features invariably allow us to infer its intention. Consider Helen, the theologically fastidious hymn-singer introduced in §2.3. If she sang the hymn without any public declaration of the reasoning which made it possible for her to do so sincerely, then a casual observer will have no way of distinguishing Helen's action from what the rest of the congregation was doing in singing the same hymn. Does that pose a problem for intentionalists? Only if they lay claim to omniscience – and there are other reasons why they should not do that. Certainly, the fact that we are unable to answer a given question in a particular set of circumstances does not mean that questions of that kind can never be answered in any circumstances. Two points can be made. First, the 'casual observer' unable to distinguish Helen's intentions was carefully selected to have no relevant background information. Replace the casual observer with a friend who has a good knowledge of Helen's theological outlook, and who has talked to her about issues relating to ecumenical theology and the individual appropriation of shared credal formulae, and you have an interpreter who will readily discern that she could not have meant what her fellow-worshippers meant, and who is well-equipped to form plausible hypotheses about the sense in which she could sing the hymn. So the hymn-singer's intention in our example is not unknowable in general, but only to an interpreter who lacks relevant information; and it would be absurd to take the least informed interpreter as the norm for interpretative theory. Of course, with regard to any ancient author we are closer to the uninformed observer than the friend. But the interpreter's dependence on knowledge about the individual in Helen's case is exceptional. For, secondly, this example has some features that are not characteristic of all linguistic behaviour. In particular, Helen was not engaged in communicating a specific theological position to others. The fact that the singing of the hymn was not (in this respect, at least) directed towards an audience accounts for the difficulty that an audience would have in construing the singer's intention. Where an audience is intentionally addressed, the intention should be easier to construe, since the relevant background information is more likely to be public.

The intentionalist does not claim, therefore, that intention is always accessible to an observer. All that need be claimed is that intention is the kind of thing that is potentially and in principle accessible to an observer. Yet the notion that there is something inherently and profoundly opaque about intentions is widespread and persistent. I shall discuss two instances, both particularly significant because each scholar, in carefully qualified ways, goes on to affirm the relevance of authorial intention to interpretation: these are not dogmatic anti-intentionalists.

R.G. Williams, a theorist of textual criticism of modern texts, says:[6]

> No one can determine exhaustively and certainly the initiatives that constitute his or her own intent .... What is unknowable on the part of the intender is in addition radically uninspectable for the construer: if intents are psychological events that are not transparent to the intender, they are fundamentally inaccessible to the mind of another.

Note that Williams starts by setting a very demanding standard: partial, provisional and avowedly fallible hypotheses are not considered; intent must be determinable *exhaustively* and *certainly*. From the uncontroversial impossibility of meeting that demand we leap disconcertingly to a blanket 'unknowable'. There then follows an argument *a fortiori*: if intentions are not knowable to the intender, they are even more unknowable to an observer – *radically* uninspectable and *fundamentally* inaccessible. Thus the failure of the intender's self-awareness to satisfy an exceptionally stringent criterion is taken as evidence of the exceptionally complete inaccessibility of intention to observers. But there must be something wrong with the argument, given the absurdity of the conclusion (in daily life, we do make plausible and often correct judgements about other people's intentions). And two of the premises seem questionable in the light of the discussion in §3.1. If intentions are not (or not just) 'psychological events' but part of the structure of overt action (iii), they are less plausibly portrayed as mysterious and inaccessible; and if we do not accept that individual agents' access to their own intentions is necessarily privileged (iv), then the argument's *a fortiori* structure falls apart.

Stephen Hinds writes in a similar vein of 'one of the most famous and broadly acknowledged impasses in twentieth-century criticism: the ultimate *unknowability* of the poet's intention', adding 'let us immediately concede the epistemological point, which is incontrovertible'.[7] The emphasis on '*unknowability*' should not distract attention from the qualifier (compare Williams' use of adverbs: exhaustively, certainly, radically, fundamentally). If Hinds is saying that a poet's (but why privilege poets? presumably, the point can be generalised: anyone's) intentions cannot be known *at all* – that they are the ultimate in unknowability – the point runs up against the same empirical objection that we brought against Williams: it is not, in fact, the case that other people's intentions are utterly unknowable. Alternatively, he might be saying that intentions can be known *up to a point*, but not *ultimately*; that is, intentions, though knowable, are only knowable in some penultimate way. In this case, the contrast would be between a knowledge that is exhaustive and certain (compare, again, Williams) and one that is partial and provisional. But then the point is pretty weak. It poses no threat to an intentionalist who claims that intentions are knowable in some degree, provisionally, fallibly .... Cautious intentionalists have nothing to fear from denials of the *ultimate* knowability of intentions; what *can* be known 'ultimately'? Still less do they have anything to fear from denials of the 'unproblematic knowability' that Hinds alludes to in the same context (p. 48 n. 62). Intentionalist or not, a classicist who is looking for unproblematic knowledge is in the wrong business.

We have, then, compelling arguments against the view that intentions can be known unproblematically or exhaustively or certainly. But that is not a view to which intentionalists are committed. And the impossibility of knowing intentions in that way is hardly distinctive. What is the contrast? Is intention an isolated blank in a tapestry of otherwise certain, complete and unproblematic knowledge of the ancient world? Obviously not: but then – what is the force of the objection?

3.3. Are intentions interesting?

An epigrapher reading an inscription needs to distinguish accidental markings on the stone from those which the mason made on purpose. Accidental marks include, for example, those produced by flaws in the stone, by slips of the mason's chisel, or by subsequent weathering and damage. Marks that are judged accidental in this sense do not provide support to the kinds of inference that can be based on marks made intentionally. For example, in the case of a much-discussed inscription recording an alliance between Athens and Egesta, different opinions about whether or not a certain mark is a trace of an originally inscribed iota or an accidental scratch yield different restorations of the name of the archon in office when the decree was passed, and thus produce a 40-year variance in the dating of the decree. That has wider implications. The inscription contains three-barred sigmas; so if it dates to the archonship of Antiphon (418/7) rather than that of Habron (458/7) it overturns the widely held but contested principle that this letter-form fell out of use in the mid-440s. That in turn would open the way to a redating of other inscriptions that have been dated solely on the basis of the three-barred sigma; and that, in turn again, might lead to significant changes in our understanding of the course of fifth-century Athenian history.[8]

In the case of the Egesta decree, the restoration of the incompletely preserved archon's name rests on indistinct traces on the stone. Often, however, an epigrapher has help in restoring missing letters or words in an inscription. Formulaic language attested in other inscriptions of a similar kind may point the way to a restoration. Faced with a resolution of 'the council and [...]', the restoration of 'the people' is not too taxing. This process might be thought a purely technical one, requiring no reference to intention. But further reflection shows that this is not the case. No inscription appears on a stone spontaneously – not even a standard formula; someone has to put it there. Unless we assume some agent (whether the person who drafted the text or the mason who inscribed it) intentionally conforming to the formula, we have no warrant for concluding that the formula appeared at that point in the complete inscription. We do not need to find independent evidence of the individual inscriber's intention in order to justify the formulaic supplement; even so, the inference that the formulaic supplement is likely to be correct implicitly commits us to claims about what was intended. The parallels that attest to the existence of the formula function as evidence of the probable intention.

3. Good intentions

The problem of restoring an original text is not limited to inscriptions. It is a problem that interpreters of classical texts have constantly to reckon with. As a result of the errors that are inevitable when a text is repeatedly copied in a manuscript tradition, classical literature is typically preserved in a form that is incomplete or inaccurate; the text has therefore to be constructed in the very process of interpretation. In textual criticism, as in epigraphy, no purely technical process is sufficient. A solution to a textual problem that is as elegant as it possibly could be in technical terms (one, for example, that keeps close to the transmitted reading and can explain economically how every manuscript variant arose) is unacceptable if it fails to provide a sense that is appropriate to the context. And this must mean: a sense that the author might have found appropriate to the context. For a text that does not express a meaning that can plausibly be attributed to the author is not a text that the author is likely to have written, no matter how appropriate that meaning might seem to us by some other criterion. To answer the question 'What is Sophocles likely to have *written* here?', we also need to ask the question 'What is Sophocles likely to have *meant* here?'

This argument assumes that the textual critic is trying to reconstruct what the author wrote. There is no absolute requirement on us to do so. For some purposes, what the author wrote is essentially irrelevant. For example, if I am interested in how *Antigone* was read in the sixteenth century I will need to know what text of the play was printed in sixteenth-century editions; whether the text in those editions corresponds to what Sophocles wrote need be of no concern to me in the context of that enquiry. But there are purposes for which it is important to know whether a given state of the text corresponds to what Sophocles wrote. I may, for example, want to use the play as evidence for fifth-century Athenian society or culture. A state of the text that arises from later miscopying or interpolation will not be relevant evidence for the fifth century. My use of the text in the context of this enquiry will therefore be compromised to the extent that I am unable to diagnose later errors and interpolations; and this will, as I have argued, involve recognising that the transmitted text fails to say anything that the author is likely to have meant.

It is worth noting that the text produced by a series of transcriptional errors is not a product of purposive action. Spontaneously generated texts are therefore not merely a thought-experiment for the classicist (just as, for the classicist, 'the text' cannot be taken as something given in advance of interpretative enquiry). A text produced by accidental errors of transcription cannot be interpreted in terms of what the author intended, since it did not have an author in the relevant sense. But we can ask what would or could have been meant by it. Indeed, we must ask that: asking that question and failing to come up with a plausible answer is perhaps the most important consideration that may drive us to conclude that the transmitted text is corrupt. We have here a particular application of a point made in §2.1 – that we can talk about the meanings that might be given to a text by hypothetical or counterfactual speakers and writers. A theory about the actual intentions of the author can only emerge from the assessment of hypotheses about what the author might have meant. But unless we are willing to adopt (however provisionally, tentatively, guardedly) some such theory, some at least of the purposes that classicists typically have in their dealings with ancient texts will remain closed to us. This should not seem surprising. The *Antigone* is the product of purposive action. It results from a series of choices made by the author, and it was the making of those choices that most immediately determined the text's structure and content. What would be surprising, surely, is if it were possible to give a satisfactory account of the text while abstracting entirely from its intentionality. A decision to exclude reference to intention from interpretation would seem perverse.

This line of argument does not assume that the author individually, or the author's intentions as such, are our primary interest. The point is simply that in order to answer the questions in which we are primarily interested we may first have to address questions in which authorial intention is implicated. A classicist might reasonably have an interest in understanding the society or culture of a particular ancient community. That is not primarily an interest in any author's intentions, but the evidence we need to satisfy that interest may depend on the answers to intentionalist questions, since failure to take account of intentions may invalidate the answers we infer to other kinds of question. (The general point that non-intentional meanings sometimes depend on intentional meanings was already made in §3.1(x).)

Suppose, for example, that we want to use Greek tragedy in the context of an enquiry into some aspect of the cultural and social world of fifth-century Athens. We observe, for instance, that tragedies often portray situations that are ethically problematic. The attempt to apply even basic principles of Greek morality (such as 'help friends, harm enemies') regularly leads to conflict, contradiction or irresolvable uncertainty. We might wish to argue, therefore, that tragedy tends to put in doubt the adequacy of these principles. And it is surely reasonable to suppose that this must disclose something distinctive and important about fifth-century Athens. A subversive, questioning dramatic form was not only tolerated, but actively promoted at publicly sponsored festivals. Why? If we can provide an explanation we may find that our understanding of fifth-century Athenian culture has been extended in a key respect. But this line of argument is flawed. All that has been established so far is that tragedy seems *to us* to put in doubt the adequacy of certain moral principles. We have not yet established anything about fifth-century Athens, beyond the fact that it produced texts that we are inclined to read in such terms. But that may simply be a fact about us and how we read. It does not in itself warrant much by way of inference about fifth-century Athens.

Consider two divergent intentionalist commentaries on the tragic phenomenon we have observed:

(a) The portrayal in tragedy of situations in which the application of basic moral principles proves problematic seems to us to put in doubt the adequacy of these principles; and this suggests that tragedians wrote (in part) to explore and critique the moral values of their society.

(b) The portrayal in tragedy of situations in which the application of basic moral principles proves problematic seems to us to put in doubt the adequacy of these principles; however, there is evidence to suggest that tragedians wrote primarily to elicit an intense emotional response.

3. Good intentions

An interpreter who adopts (a) can legitimately draw the kind of inference about fifth-century Athens that was previously blocked. On this view, a dramatic form that was *designed* to be subversive was promoted at public festivals; we do, therefore, need to develop a model of the social and cultural context that explains why the community sponsored behaviour that was purposefully critical of its prevailing ideology. (One possible explanation is that Athenian audiences did not realise that this is what tragedians were trying to do. But as I have already indicated (§1.1), I do not find the hypothesis of a systematic divergence between tragedians and their audiences a very tempting one. In the absence of evidence to support that view, we would do better to assume some correlation between intention and reception, and seek a socio-cultural explanation.) By contrast, for an interpreter holding to (b), nothing of the kind needs to be explained: for on this hypothesis, tragedy was not subversive. What would then need to be explained is something quite different: why did fifth-century Athenians not see tragedy in a way that strikes us as obvious? That question needs to be approached with caution. We should not allow it to smuggle in a tacit assumption that there is something *odd* about the Athenian perspective, as if our way of seeing things was natural or inevitable. The need for explanation is symmetrical: why do *we* imagine that something is obvious when it has not been obvious to others? But provided that this tacit assumption is removed, asking the question may well lead us to a better understanding of fifth-century Athenian culture (it will certainly throw light on its distance from our own). But it will lead to a *different* understanding from the one to which the first argument sketched out here would have led. So the inferences we can draw from tragedy about its social and cultural context are not independent of the hypotheses we form about what the tragedians were intentionally doing.

The two hypotheses are not mutually exclusive, of course, and it might be argued that there is no need to choose between them. Why not combine them?

(a+b) The portrayal in tragedy of situations in which the application of basic moral principles proves problematic seems to us to put in doubt the adequacy of these principles; this suggests that tragedians wrote (in part) to explore and critique the moral values of their society; but there is also evidence to suggest that tragedians wrote primarily to elicit an intense emotional response.

That is a perfectly coherent theory. But we do have to choose whether to combine the hypotheses in this way or not. If we do choose to combine them we automatically rule out other members of the field of possibilities. And the field is far from having been exhausted by the two hypotheses so far considered. For example:

(c) The portrayal in tragedy of situations in which the application of basic moral principles proves problematic seems to us to put in doubt the adequacy of these principles; however, there is evidence the tragedians were writing (in part) to illustrate and reinforce the moral values of their society.

This hypothesis can claim a good deal of support from what

3. Good intentions

was said about tragedy in antiquity, as can (b). So the combination of (b) and (c) has something to be said for it, as well.[9] There are, of course, many other possibilities. The point here is not which hypothesis is correct. It is simply that there are choices to be made, and different choices will lead us to different conclusions about the cultural context.

Can we decline these choices? The proposition that 'tragedians wrote in part to critique current ideology' warrants inferences about fifth-century Athenian culture that are not warranted by 'tragedians produced texts that can be read as critiques of current ideology'. As we have already seen, the latter proposition may only tell us something about the results of applying current exegetical techniques. So if we refuse to take any view about what tragedians were doing, we risk denying ourselves the possibility of exploring this area of Athenian culture. Of course, if we conclude that we cannot tell what tragedians were doing, we will also find that possibility denied us. But we cannot reach that conclusion – except dogmatically – unless we are willing to ask the question and try to answer it.

The choices we make will lead us, not only upwards to an understanding of the cultural context, but downwards to a more detailed understanding of individual texts. An interpreter who holds to (a) will focus on evidence of problems in applying moral principles as part of the point of any play, and the elements of the play that are highlighted as thematically and structurally significant will reflect that focus. An interpreter holding to (b), however, will not see those problems as part of the point of the play, and will accordingly highlight other features as thematically and structurally significant. That does not mean that this interpreter will ignore the problems of moral conflict and confusion; but they will be seen as playing a different role (for example, as part of the dramatist's technique for placing characters in painful situations that will excite a sympathetic response in the audience). Nor does it mean that the moral issues are of subordinate interest to the interpreter. It may be that the interpreter is interested in tragedy precisely because of the light which its dramatisation of moral conflict throws on ancient ethics. The point is rather that enquirers should be able to distinguish between the focus of their own interest and the focus of interest of the texts with which they engage in the course of their enquiry. More precisely, enquirers *need* to be able to make this distinction if they are to make well-informed and accurate use of the text as evidence in the context of their enquiry. (Consider how the experiment described at the end of §3.1 was vitiated by a failure to take account of the perspective of the children involved.)

It will (I hope) be obvious by now that my commitment to intentionalism is of a limited and pragmatic kind. It is not motivated, for example, by the concerns which exercised Hirsch, who argued for authorial intention as a norm of interpretation on the grounds that it provides the only possible solution to the problem of determinacy and validity.[10] I do not believe that intentions *are* fully determinate (§3.1(vi)), and do not see determinacy of meaning as something inherently valuable anyway. Rather, I think that questions about authorial intention are worth asking because they are relevant to satisfying a variety of interests that people have in texts.

My argument so far has concentrated on indirect relevance.

3. Good intentions

That is, I have considered ways in which asking intentionalist questions may be instrumentally useful in the conduct of other, ulterior enquiries. Nothing said so far depends on seeing authorial intention as something of potential interest in itself. But that has been a purely tactical omission, and I will conclude this section by briefly filling in the gap. In many social interactions, it may be true that my only interest is in the outcome. The point of my conversation with the fishmonger (§3.1(vi)) is to buy a pound or so of squid for a reasonable price; so long as this goal is achieved, I will be satisfied. I need take no more interest in the fishmonger's intentions (nor he in mine) than is required to facilitate the transaction. But there are often reasons why in practice we do take more interest in each other than that. This may be the case even in a seemingly routine piece of business: perhaps I know from previous experience that this fishmonger has a sense of humour, and is likely to liven up the transaction with a sly joke. Likewise, if Aristophanes was good at making jokes, it is reasonable (if you like jokes) to take an interest in the jokes he made (not just in whatever jokes we can make out of his words). If Aristotle was good at framing arguments, it is reasonable (if you are interested in argument) to take an interest in Aristotle's arguments (not just in whatever arguments we can hang on his words). If Sophocles was good at writing tragedy it is reasonable (if you enjoy tragedy) to take an interest in the tragedies that Sophocles composed (not just in whatever tragedies we can construct from his words). It would surely be impoverishing to exclude such interests. But there is a deeper form of impoverishment at stake, as well. In §2.2 we made the point about the power of human curiosity in driving enquiry. Would it not be arbitrary to exclude an interest in individual human beings from the scope of human curiosity?

3.4. In defence of reading

But surely there are other things to do, things that are much more exciting? 'The critic asks neither the author nor the text about their intentions but simply beats the text into a shape which will serve his own purpose.'[11] The critic here is Richard Rorty's 'strong textualist' or 'strong misreader', who is 'in it for what he can get out of it, not for the satisfaction of getting something right' (p. 152).

Rorty goes on to suggest (p. 153) that 'from a full-fledged pragmatist point of view, there is no interesting difference between tables and texts, between protons and poems. To a pragmatist, these are *all* just permanent possibilities for use.' This is a puzzling statement, precisely from a pragmatist point of view. For there are many interesting differences between these various things. In particular, there are striking differences between them with regard to *what* possibilities for use each presents – try getting four people to sit round a proton to play a game of cards. The differences in potential uses correlate with structural differences in the objects themselves. So it makes no sense to say they are *just* possibilities for use; they could not *be* useful if they did not have a particular structure independent of and antecedent to our purposes. Moreover, there is another difference between a table and a proton: one is an artefact, and one is not. So in this respect tables resemble poems and texts, and we can talk about them in terms that do not apply to protons (what is the purpose of this table? why was it made like this? what ideological message does its design convey?). The world is more interestingly varied than Rorty's dichotomy, let alone its dissolution into an undifferentiated mass of things that are 'just' permanent possibilities for use, allows.

Four years later Rorty was able to identify one – though still only one – interesting difference between tables and texts, protons and poems (the dichotomy has now been generalised into one between 'lumps' and 'texts'):[12]

> There obviously *is* something called 'the author's intention' which we can and do use to give sense to Level II in the case of texts, but which we cannot use to give sense to Level II in the case of lumps. The *only* interesting difference between texts and lumps is that we know how to form and defend hypotheses about the author's intentions in the one case but not in the other.

It would no doubt be unfair to assume that it was only in the interval between the two essays that Rorty began to find a possible source of interest in hypotheses about author's intentions; perhaps there was a touch of provocative hyperbole in the earlier formulations. But the juxtaposition helps to expose, even so, how seriously flawed those earlier formulations were. The notion that asking about the intentions of an author and serving one's own purpose are mutually exclusive is wholly misconceived. If, for whatever reason, the critic finds the author's intentions interesting, then asking about them *is* serving the critic's own purpose (a point made already in §2.2). In that case, too, the satisfaction of getting something right *is* one of the things a critic can get out of it. Moreover, getting it right may have consequential benefits; even trying to get it right might have benefits.

(By 'getting it right' I mean, simply, successfully answering whatever question you find you have reason to ask. In Rorty's usage 'getting it right' seems to connote getting to some *ultimate* hidden truth. For example, the 'weak textualist ... thinks that each work has its own vocabulary, its own secret code' and wants 'a privileged vocabulary ... which gets to the essence of its object' (p. 152). But I cannot see any reason why Rorty's opponents should acquiesce in this arbitrary loading of the argument against them.)

This is not to deny that the strong misreader's project is a coherent and legitimate one. 'Meaning', in the account I have given (§2.1), has no intrinsic meaning; what counts as meaning depends on the questions we are asking, and 'What useful or pleasing shapes can I beat this text into?' is a question it makes sense to ask. (I did a bit of this myself in the course of §1.4, exploiting Don Fowler's words for my own expository convenience.) My argument is simply that this is not the only question it makes sense to ask, and not the only question that may be worth asking. By way of recommending the interpretative project of strong misreading Rorty offers us a vision of the creative misreader whose imposition of shape on the text 'gives us a new vocabulary which enables us to do a lot of new and marvellous things' (p.153). This outcome would no doubt make it all worthwhile. But it is not the only possible outcome. The strong misreader proceeds by 'imposing a vocabulary ... on the text' (p. 151); he 'has his own vocabulary, and doesn't worry about whether anybody shares it' (p. 152). This offers us a glimpse of a less appealing vision: the *uncreative* mis-reader, whose imposition of shape on the text obsessively reproduces an existing vocabulary that he or she happens to be attached to – one that does not necessarily enable us to do anything fruitful at all. In such hands, cultural dialogue may undergo a depressing transformation. It threatens to become a monologue delivered by the kind of bore who turns everything said by other people into a pretext for further rehearsing his own preoccupations.

The creation of a new and marvellously fruitful vocabulary is not a common occurrence. But that does not mean that we can only reproduce existing vocabularies. Vocabularies can be changed incrementally from within; and for most of us, that modest aspiration is more realistic than Rorty's visionary misreading. One thing we can do in pursuit of this goal is to talk to other people – or, more precisely, *listen* to them. Exposure to their different vocabularies may provide us with resources to reflect critically on the current state of our own, and to envisage alternatives to it. Exposure to the more radically different vocabularies of people in the past may provide us with correspondingly more radical alternatives, and more powerful tools for self-critical reflection – if we are willing to listen. The strong misreader has decided not to listen. More historically minded approaches to interpretation, including the intentionalist project defended in this chapter, are willing to make the attempt.

4

Contexts and consequences

Listening to voices from the past may provide us with resources for critical reflection on the current state of our own vocabularies, our ways of talking and thinking. I shall return to that idea towards the end of this final chapter. But there are questions to consider first as to how the attempt to listen to past voices should be undertaken. I shall assume, in the light of the preceding chapter, that our approach to interpretation will include (among others) questions about authors' intentions. But the pluralist framework developed in Chapter 2 remains in place, and much of what I say will also be relevant to historically oriented interpretative projects that prefer not to characterise themselves in intentionalist terms.

Texts are always read in context. That is inevitable, since the process of interpretation itself necessarily takes place in some context. We have already seen one aspect of the constitutive importance of the context of interpretation: it is this context that makes the text significant and thereby gives content to the notion of 'meaning' (§2.1, §2.4). But the historical orientation of our interpretative project also requires us to pay attention to the context in which the text was composed. This, too, follows from the preceding analysis: the author is embedded in a social context, and can only be understood in relation to that context (§3.1(x)-(xi)). As will become clear, intermediary contexts – those of the text's transmission and reception – have a contribution to make to our enquiry as well. In this chapter, I shall have something to say about all these contexts, taking the context of interpretation first. But before that something more needs to be said about the structure of enquiry in general.

4.1. Preconceptions

In §3.1(iii) I suggested that it was misleading when Oliver Lyne described as a 'preconception' the view (held by some) that *Aeneid* 6.460 was not intended to allude significantly to Catullus 66.39; it is, I suggested, simply and innocuously a conception, a conclusion reached in the course of enquiry. But an interpreter who has come to hold this view will probably be guided by it in her further exploration of the *Aeneid*. So the conclusion, once reached, is certainly likely to *become* a preconception for the purpose of future enquiries. Does it then cease to be innocuous?

There would indeed be a problem if the preconception were immutably fixed (especially when, as may well be the case in this example, it is wrong). But there is no reason why it need be fixed. It is always possible that the interpreter will come across some further consideration that encourages her to revisit and revise her (always interim) conclusions. This would, for one thing, be a natural result of the process of discussion and disagreement which we considered in Chapter 1. Suppose our interpreter reads Lyne's article and is impressed by it. She is unlikely, perhaps, to take over its conclusions intact; after all, she is asking questions about Virgil's intentions, as Lyne is not, and that alone will require some adjustment. But the textual and intertextual patterns that Lyne picks out might prompt a change in the answer she gives to her own intentionalist questions. If she finds Lyne's analysis plausible, it would be reasonable for her to conjecture that Virgil intentionally gave Aeneas words to speak that – unintentionally on Aeneas' part – underscored the tragedy of Dido's death. (Let us note in passing that her understanding of the poem is more likely to be influenced by Lyne's concrete engagement with the text than by his theoretical objections to her intentionalist project. This has some relevance to the question of the status of theory, raised in §1.3, as well as illustrating the point, made in §2.1, that interpretative discussion may be fruitful even when conducted across a theoretical divide.)

Another thing that contributes to the mutability of interim conclusions is the fact that interpretation does not proceed in straight lines. In §3.3 we saw how interpretation might move from a general proposition about the nature of a genre (for example, what kind of thing fifth-century tragedians were, broadly speaking, doing) up towards an understanding of the genre's social and cultural context and down towards an understanding of textual detail. But that is an over-simplified picture. In reality there is a constant movement back and forth between many different levels of analysis. When we interpret a text, our understanding of its contemporary context is one important input; but when we try to understand the context, our reading of contemporary texts is an important input in turn. So text and context are dynamically interrelated: our construction of each modifies the other. Likewise, our interpretation of a text as a whole depends on our reading of its parts, and our reading of its parts depends on our reading of the whole. So further discoveries at any one level can react on the interim conclusions reached at any other level, and may lead to their revision.

The history of my own reading of Aristophanes may illustrate the process. I once saw him as a political poet in a strong sense – as a conservative who sought to use comedy to influence the political behaviour of his audiences. But as time went on I found it increasingly difficult to reconcile that view with what I seemed to encounter in the comedies themselves. Consider Bdelycleon's speech in the agon of *Wasps* (650-724). My strongly political perception of Aristophanes suggested that I should be reading the speech as a pointed critique of the system of popular juries and pay for jury-service; in fact, I found myself more strongly impressed by the speech's populist mockery of the political elite, and by its complaints that ordinary people have no power and are insufficiently rewarded. This and similar observations eventually persuaded me that a more coherent account of the comedies could be developed on the assumption that Aristophanes generally used political material to amuse his audience, with a view to winning first prize in the comic competition but without a political intent that reached beyond the theatre.[1] There are a number of things to be observed, in passing, about this conclusion. First, the attunement of comedy's political content to its audience makes Aristophanes' own political outlook opaque: there is no intrinsic connection between intentionalist interpretation and a biographical interest in the author. Secondly, this reading does not sever connections between comedy and its political and social context: my conclusion was, on the contrary, that it brings to light an ambivalent attitude towards the wealthy on the part of Aristophanes' audience, highlighting tensions within democratic ideology, and that it tells us something about the democracy's control of the theatre. Thirdly, this account of comedy offers a high-level generalisation that may guide detailed interpretation, but does not rigidly constrain it: it leaves open the possibility that Aristophanes did not always conform to the general rule. I suggested, for example, that the parabasis of *Frogs* may be an exception; the political material there does not seem to have been developed with a view to amusement, and the possibility of genuinely political intent has therefore to be considered. The willingness to accommodate such exceptions is not an arbitrary *ad hoc* device. I have argued (§3.1(xii)) that language is always incomplete and open to transformation; not every possibility in the field of potential meanings is equally accessible, but none is utterly beyond reach. The same will apply to the possibilities accessible within a given genre. The flexibility in application which this opens up adds yet another element of fluidity to any preconception.

Our preconceptions may also be destabilised by changes in background assumptions. Again, my own experience may provide an illustration. I have already mentioned (§1.5) my initially incredulous reaction to the thesis that Pindar's victory odes were composed for solo performance. That epinician was a form of choral poetry was a well-known fact that I had no reason to question. Indeed, I knew perfectly well that internal evidence confirmed it: there are many passages in Pindar that refer to a group of young men (the chorus) singing the victory ode. But then I reread the poems, and noticed that the young men are described as a *kômos*, not as a chorus; was it legitimate to equate the two? Moreover, though the young men sing and dance (as one would expect members of the mobile celebration known as *kômos* to do) the poems do not explicitly confirm that what they were singing was the commissioned, formal victory ode; that was an inference drawn in the light of the prior assumption of choral performance. So my previous understanding had a self-confirming tendency: the premise that the poems were choral encouraged me to read them in a way that furnished evidence that they were choral. That loop had now been broken. One factor in this breach was my awareness that the choral interpretation had been challenged. As I reread the poems I was now posing a question that I had not previously thought to ask: 'If we did not know that the poems were written for choral performance, how might we understand them?' But others have reread the poems in the light of the challenge without finding sufficient reason to revise their opinion. An additional factor operative in my own case was the fact that, in the course of writing a book review a few years earlier, I had mentally flagged the relationship between epinician poetry and *kômos* as a topic worth investigating at some future date; so I was more alert to the possible relevance of references to the *kômos* than I might otherwise have been. Moreover, I had long been dissatisfied with the notion of the 'encomiastic future' (a supposedly conventional use of the future tense to refer to, for example, the performance of a song in the present), and was open to a new approach that would turn these into genuine futures. There were attractions, therefore, in a reading that took references to young

4. Contexts and consequences

men singing *other* songs as a technique for embedding the victory ode in a performance context that as a matter of course would include such singing. That in turned opened up the possibility that the commissioned victory ode was (sometimes? often? usually? always?) composed for solo performance. I could no longer assume that we *knew* that the poems were chorally performed. Admittedly, it does not follow that they were performed solo; the *kômos* as the context for performance is consistent with performance by a chorus, and it is possible that in due course someone will provide compelling arguments to show that choral performance was the norm after all. If so, the process of discussion and disagreement will have proved its value, helping to put a long-standing consensus on a firmer footing than it previously had; and the option of understanding passages that used to be read as self-referential allusions to the ode's own performance as references connecting the ode to its komastic performance context will still be open to us.[2]

This discussion of background assumptions has brought us back to a theme we touched on in §1.3. New information has to be integrated into a network of existing beliefs, and the significance of that information is not intrinsic but arises from its relations within the network. What we learn depends on what we already believe. Enquiry is therefore always prejudiced, to take up the provocative term which Hans-Georg Gadamer used to formulate the point. This concept of prejudice does not imply, however, that thought is always rigidly constrained by obstinately held dogmas. The point is rather that in any enquiry we have to proceed from where we are. How else could we proceed at all? If we assumed nothing, we would have no way of framing questions or making sense of evidence. So it would be absurd to deplore the prejudicial structure of understanding; it is what makes understanding possible. Prejudice (in this sense) is not a defect of enquiry, but its precondition. If the pejorative connotations of 'prejudice' prove too distracting, one might think instead of prior judgements: any judgement one makes will rest on prior judgements.[3] Or one could speak of preliminary judgements, and thus mark their provisionality. The enquirer's task cannot be the impossible one of becoming unprejudiced; but it does not follow that our prejudices must be accepted uncritically or that they are immune to revision. Our thinking must always start somewhere, but that does not mean there is any starting-point to which our thinking is inexorably bound; we can change our presuppositions. The task of enquiry is therefore not the elimination of prejudice, but the critical modification of prejudice from within.

One image often used in this connection is that of 'horizon'. A visual horizon determines what we can see, but is not fixed; as we move, the horizon changes. The metaphorical horizon within which enquiry is conducted likewise determines what we can see, but is open to change. The horizon changes, at the minimum, when something new comes into view – that is, when we acquire additional information. But this image has its limitations. Our experiences do not always conform to what is anticipated by existing beliefs, and we then have to make a critical assessment of the new information ('that can't be true!') or of the prior beliefs with which it conflicts ('so I must have been wrong to think ...'). The horizon metaphor does not adequately capture this idea of a self-adjusting system that actively evaluates and organises knowledge in response to new input. The metaphor of a web or network, which had the merit of offering an alternative to that of knowledge as a founded structure (§1.4), also fails here. It does succeed in capturing the inter-relatedness of our knowledge, but is too static. Our knowledge of the world is a continual *process* of self-adjustment, prompted by the need to assimilate and make sense of new experience. The web image simply isolates a moment in that process.

For this process of self-adjustment to be possible our commitments (beliefs, theories, hypotheses, conjectures ...) must be open to revision. But an interesting problem confronts us here. If our commitments are too open to revision, enquiry will be thwarted in another way. If we were not willing to hold on to a hypothesis in the face of apparently unfavourable evidence and counter-arguments, we would never find what could be said in its defence (the counter-counter-arguments). So there is good reason not to change our position at the first sign of trouble; a degree of tenacity is prudent. Equally, in establishing a position in the first place we must be prepared to go beyond the evidence. If we did not, we would never get anywhere, since in the study of the ancient world the available evidence is always incomplete. So we need to make judgements that overreach the evidence; a degree of boldness is essential. But we should not be *too* bold (bold to the point of rashness) or *too* tenacious (tenacious to the point of obstinacy). Needless to say, there is no rule that determines how we are to judge the golden mean of boldness and tenacity. Once again, we have to acknowledge the inevitability of disagreement.

4.2. The context of interpretation

We have already seen the importance of reflecting on the questions we are asking (§1.3, §2.2). The analysis of enquiry and its prejudicial structure in §4.1 shows the importance of reflecting also on the network of assumptions that the interpreter brings to the process of interpretation – and, more widely, on the assumptions of the community within whose ongoing discussion the interpreter works. For these assumptions are crucial in determining how a text will be understood. The horizon that they establish is at once an indispensable enabling structure for interpretation, and a standing obligation to engage in self-critical reflection.

This brings us back by another route to the conclusion we reached about consensus in §1.5: consensus is essential, and yet should make us wary. But, as we also noted there, our background assumptions (the things we attend *from*) lack salience. If we take something tacitly for granted, how do we know that we have done so? It is not easy to become aware of what is implicitly obvious. And if we do become aware of something that seems obvious, how are we to achieve a critical stance towards it? It is not easy, either, to distance ourselves from our own assumptions, combining actual commitment with hypothetical detachment ('I believe such-and-such to be the case: but how would things appear if I did not?'). So the process of self-critical reflection is difficult. It is also always incomplete. Total transparency to oneself is impossible in principle; and we cannot adopt a critical stance towards all our assumptions at once, since we would then have no position from which to pose critical questions. It would be pointless, therefore, to strive to eliminate the context of interpretation. We cannot exempt ourselves from being situated in a context. But that does not mean that there is any particular context in which we are necessarily situated; we can *change* our situation. (This is the same conclusion that we reached in §4.1 about our preconceptions.) Trying to understand our situation and be critical of it is one way of changing that situation, and the fact that this process is always incomplete is no reason to play down its importance. After all the process of becoming better informed is also always incomplete, and that is no recommendation of ignorance.

It is here that intermediary contexts have an important contribution to make. One of the things that may inform the process of self-critical reflection is an awareness of the history of the reception of the texts in which we are interested – the diverse ways in which they have been read over the years. Our own ways of reading the text are the product of that history, and to see how we reached our present situation may help us understand what that situation actually is. Furthermore, seeing our current situation as the outcome of a historical process may help us recognise its contingency. In this way what we would otherwise take for granted will become more salient, and may lose its appearance of inevitability. That is not to say that such historical perspectives will compel us to abandon our current ways of reading. They do not even place us under an obligation to do so. All ways of reading are historically contingent, so the mere fact of contingency can carry no such obligation. (We saw in §1.5 that the contingency and mutability of our current beliefs does not oblige us to abandon them.)

But acquiring this kind of perspective empowers us to question our ways of reading, and provides a lever that may encourage such questioning. If we want to retain a particular way of reading, *why*? The automatic assertion of the superiority of our present starting-point is uncritical. We need to justify the continuation of our current assumptions in the face of the alternatives which the history of reception brings to light.

This point, too, can be connected with what was said about disagreement in Chapter 1. Studying the history of reception extends the benefit of discussion with others (§1.3) by bringing us into dialogue with people whose views are more radically different from our own, and (in particular) with people who are not committed to the assumptions that we share with our contemporaries. In the face of the tendency of a consensus to entrench itself and render itself invisible, the study of the history of reception can provide a rich source of disagreement, and thus a stimulus to enquiry and discovery. Just as encountering the disagreement of contemporary colleagues may have an impact on individual bias, so encountering the disagreement of past colleagues may have an impact on the biases we share with our contemporaries. Of course, this will only happen if we are willing to respect views that are unfamiliar and uncongenial. An interpretation of Greek tragedy from (say) the sixteenth century is likely to strike us as unsatisfactory, for the simple reason that it rests on assumptions that we do not share. But unless we are complacent, we should then seek to evaluate those assumptions; and it is not enough to evaluate them unfavourably on the grounds that the interpretations they produce strike us as unsatisfactory – that would be arguing in a tight and vicious circle.

4. Contexts and consequences

4.3. Contexts of composition

In §1.5 we mentioned Aristodemus of Nysa, who suggested that Homer was a Roman. At first sight that theory is bizarre to the point of madness. How could anyone have put it forward? When we realise that Aristodemus spent time in Rome as tutor to the sons of Pompey the Great, one explanation suggests itself: perhaps it was an attempt to flatter his Roman patron. On this view we should accept at face value the theory's apparent lack of intelligibility. Proposing the theory can be understood as a piece of career-advancement on Aristodemus' part, but the theory itself was an opportunistic improvisation with no intrinsic rationale. Yet Aristodemus was a respected scholar in his own day, and he could hardly have been indifferent to the reception of his theory among his Greek professional peers; and it is in fact Greek sources that have preserved what little we know of his suggestion – there is no evidence that Romans found it interesting at all. If we are open to the possibility that what seems nonsensical to us might have made sense against a different set of background assumptions, it may prove possible to render the theory itself intelligible. We will note the long-standing interest, taken up by Hellenistic scholarship, in Homer's place of origin, and the wide range of speculative solutions that were on offer – including a number of exotic ones (such as Egypt). We will note, too, the Hellenistic interest in ethnography, with its attempts to link different peoples on the basis of supposedly shared customs; the theory (defended on that very basis by Dionysius of Halicarnassus) that the Romans were Greeks;

111

and the theory (prominent in first-century linguistic scholarship) that Latin was a Greek dialect. Against this background, Aristodemus' suggestion begins to seem less crazy. If we accept the challenge posed by the notion of a Roman Homer, we advance our understanding – not (obviously) of Homer, but of Aristodemus and his world.[4]

This example provides an illustration of the importance of understanding the context in which a text was composed. This is not simply its *objective* context; as we saw in §2.1, what is crucial in communication is the context that is intersubjectively shared between author and audience, utterer and addressee. The 'objective' context (or, more precisely, what we take the objective context to have been) may indeed be relevant for our overall description of an utterance, but it is the intersubjective context that is interpretatively relevant. Of course, there is sometimes a failure of intersubjectivity (recall the experiment described at the end of §3.1). The utterer speaks to an addressee conceived in a certain way, but it is an open question whether this conception is accurate, and it is an open question too whether the addressee in turn correctly grasps the standpoint of the utterer. From an intentionalist point of view, therefore, it would be most exact to say that the context that is decisive for interpretation is that which the utterer assumed to be shared (or sharable: the point of the qualification will I hope be clear by the end of this section) with the audience addressed.

This approach allows us to get a degree of control on the potentially endless task of understanding a text's context of composition. Consider, for example, tragedy and comedy in late fifth-century Athens. Tragedies and comedies were performed in the same city at the same time, to the same audiences in the same theatres at the same festivals. So in one sense of 'context' there was no difference between them. In another sense, however, the context of tragic and comic performances differed radically. The difference lay in the different sets of assumptions and expectations which the dramatists and their audiences brought to the composition and reception of the two kinds of play. For the purposes of contextualisation, therefore, we should not look first to the totality of the contextual culture. Indeed, that very notion is a questionable one: cultures are not organic totalities. It would be more realistic to think of a culture as comprising an imperfectly defined bundle of partially related, partially self-contained practices, displaying complex patterns of resemblance, divergence and even contradiction. It is the context defined by a particular cultural practice ('context of situation') that is most immediately relevant to interpretation, rather than the broader context ('context of culture'). That is not to deny the relevance of information from the larger social and cultural context to the understanding of a particular cultural practice; the point is rather that this relevance is always mediated by the context of situation. This gives context of situation a fundamental role in interpretation: if we are trying to contextualise tragedy, the fact that it is *tragedy* that we are trying to contextualise is crucial, and it is rash to assume that we already know what its implications are. Here, as urgently as anywhere, our prior judgements merit careful reflection and, if necessary, reconstruction.

In the rest of this section, therefore, I shall concentrate on context in this more restricted sense – on the range of background assumptions most immediately accessible and relevant in a given type of situation. I must first explain my use of certain terms. I use 'genre' to designate a class of texts presupposing a broadly common set of assumptions. This view of genre must be distinguished from the transcultural notion according to which (for example) *Antigone* and *Lear* are both instances of the genre 'tragedy'. Genre, in my sense, is a historically situated textual practice. I shall use 'poetics' to designate the system of assumptions underlying the composition and reception of texts of a given genre in this sense. (Some find the term 'poetics' distracting, since I do not limit its application to poetry, or even to the kinds of text that we might call 'literary' or 'artistic'. But I have not thought of a better one, and can plead the etymological link to the Greek *poiein*, 'make, construct', by way of excuse.) So in §3.3 the various broad characterisations of what tragedians were, in general, up to functioned as (admittedly crude and incomplete) placeholders for components of a poetics of the genre Greek tragedy.

The basic premise of this concept of poetics is that any public textual practice will rest on assumptions in some measure shared by those who participate in it, whether as producers or as recipients of the texts in question (that is, as authors or as audiences). This premise does not in any way predetermine what those shared assumptions are, or how tightly they constrain the production and reception of texts within the genre. Any established practice must fall between the impossible extremes of complete indeterminacy (which would leave it with no distinguishable identity) and complete determinacy (which would make it communicatively useless). But where on

4. Contexts and consequences

the continuum between those extremes any given genre falls is a question that must be determined empirically.

The shared assumptions of a genre will relate in part to the ways in which meaning can be realised in textual form, but also and more fundamentally to what meanings are available for realisation – the genre's meaning-potential. Genre is thus primarily a semantic concept. It could be said, therefore, that genre determines the range of available meanings; but this formulation may be misleading. The point that language does not determine what we *can* say (§3.1(xii)) must be applied here, too. It is not the case, for example, that someone preaching a sermon in church *cannot* tell obscene jokes. But a preacher who did so would be going against what we take to be shared assumptions about this genre, and we would look for some special point in this violation of expectations, as we probably would not if the same jokes had been told in a stand-up comedy routine. (It is also true that we could make various descriptive and evaluative observations about such a sermon that did not depend on identifying the intention behind the violation: see §2.4, §3.1(ix)-(x).) As we noted in §4.1 in connection with the nature of Aristophanic comedy, the possibilities accessible within the conventions (we might now say, poetics) of a genre have in common with language in general a basic incompleteness and open-endedness. A genre's meaning-potential is thus a field of possibilities within which a speaker or writer makes choices, a field that is both open-ended (there is no absolute limit to the range of meanings available) and structured (not all meanings are equally accessible, and the choice of a relatively inaccessible meaning may therefore pose an interpretative challenge in itself).

The open-endedness of meaning-potential entails that there is always scope for an element of creativity or improvisation in any use of language (§3.1(xii)). So the intersubjective context that is essential to understanding may not be fully laid down in advance. Some antecedent common ground must be assumed, but more may be mapped out in the process of interpretation itself. This is a common enough phenomenon in everyday conversation. When Eric says, 'We won't have dinner at Fin de Siècle tonight – Fiona hates seafood', adequate understanding requires a mutual awareness that Fin de Siècle is a seafood restaurant. But that mutual awareness need not exist in advance: it can be constructed inferentially in trying to make sense of what has been said. This is why I spoke earlier of a context that is assumed to be shared or *sharable*. It follows in turn that generic assumptions are not necessarily static: creative exploitations may (depending on their reception) change the shared background assumptions to which subsequent texts are addressed. Indeed, the very notion of a historically situated practice implies an evolving tradition.

The mutability of genre means that the reconstruction of a genre's poetics cannot be independent of the interpretation of the texts of that genre. We should think instead of a dialectical interdependence: a poetics is inferred from the interpretation of texts; the texts are interpreted with the aid of the poetics. The point is a familiar one: as we saw in §4.1, there are many such reciprocities as interpretation moves backwards and forwards between different levels of analysis. Interpretation rests, not on a single hermeneutic circle, but on a system of interlocking circles.

4.4. The challenge of ancient interpretation

One task, then, for a historically oriented interpretative project is to achieve some measure of understanding of the assumptions shared by native participants in the composition
and reception of texts in a given situation type. How are we
go about this? Clearly, we will be dependent for the most part
on careful observation of the practice of the composers of
texts, as evidenced by the texts they composed. But what we
are observing was a two-sided process: it involved reception as
well as composition. It is worth asking, therefore, whether
there is anything to be gained from studying evidence for the
receptive side of the communicative relationship between
author and audience. Such evidence might include explicit
discussion in ancient literary criticism and theory. For example, a reader who is interested in Greek tragedy, but who
starts from the assumption that he does not know what
Greek tragedy was for or how it worked, might think it
sensible to seek what help he can from anyone who was
better placed to know. Someone like Aristotle, an intelligent
and well-informed observer culturally less distanced from
tragedy than modern readers, might seem to fit the bill. Hence
it could be argued that Aristotle's thinking that errors of
judgement with disastrous consequences are important in tragedy carries a kind of evidential weight that my (or any of my
contemporaries') thinking so does not. Or, to take another
example, the theorisation of techniques of intentional ambiguity in Quintilian and other ancient rhetoricians could be held

117

to strengthen the hand of interpreters who detect such ambiguity in Virgil.[5]

The consequences of accepting that premise are by no means straightforward. We can never guarantee that any ancient critic or commentator is giving us the information we seek. Perhaps his view is idiosyncratic, and unrepresentative of the assumptions shared by authors and well-informed audiences. Or perhaps he has failed to report his own, perfectly representative assumptions accurately; the lack of self-transparency is something we have noted in another context (§3.1(iv)). Or perhaps the context and purpose of his report have produced a particular slant or selectivity that makes it deeply misleading; ancient critics and commentators did not set out to answer the questions to which we are seeking answers. Considerations such as these would apply even under optimum conditions. But we are far from enjoying optimum conditions. Strictly contemporary evidence (evidence drawn directly from the context in which the putative shared assumptions were shared) is generally lacking; most ancient criticism works at a certain temporal and cultural distance from the texts on which it focuses.

So it is obvious that there are many grounds for caution; but they are not, in my judgement, grounds for abandoning the basic idea. There are two points. First, and negatively, it should be stressed that identifying sources of potential difficulty in generalised terms is not enough to establish an actual difficulty in a particular instance. Since I am fallible, it is obviously likely that there are errors in this book; but only the laziest sceptic would imagine that making this point was a sufficient rebuttal of any particular statement contained in it. Secondly, and positively, our primary interest here is not in a particular critic's interpretation of a particular text, but in the assumptions underlying many different interpretations and in the common features which they share. Suppose that we can identify tendencies that are consistent across many different sources (and sources with many different kinds of purpose), that persist over an extended period, and that converge with conclusions that can be drawn from other levels of analysis. The evidence that we then have will not indeed be complete and unproblematic (evidence in the study of the ancient world is *never* complete or unproblematic); but it would need to be taken seriously.

Whether such tendencies can be identified is a question on which disagreement (needless to say) is possible. I believe that they can, and that there are important things to learn from ancient criticism. And precisely because I see it as a potentially rewarding but under-exploited resource, this use of ancient criticism in poetics is something on which I have laid programmatic emphasis – an emphasis that has sometimes been misunderstood. Denis Feeney speaks of 'Heath's Law' (p. 303): 'the claim that ancient testimony is our sole legitimate interpretative key' in the study of ancient texts.[6] But this is not a claim that I have ever made. To support the attribution Feeney quotes a passage from my *Poetics of Greek Tragedy* that seems to me to say something importantly different (it asserts the *relative* advantage of exploiting this resource as against its neglect), and that has been extracted from a context wholly inconsistent with the claim attributed to me (it comes, in fact, from a summary review of the problematic nature of the ancient testimony available to us, and its place within interlocking systems of different kinds of evidence). If I were to formulate 'Heath's Law', therefore, it would be to the effect that we are likely to achieve a better understanding of ancient texts (or, more precisely, better answers to the kinds of question that I am asking about ancient texts) if we allow a sustained but critical use of ancient testimony to inform our reconstruction of the assumptions about literary form and function underlying the composition of those texts than if we rely on assumptions about literary form and function developed without sustained reference to ancient testimony.

Heath's Heath's Law is obviously a more liberal (as well as a more verbose) piece of legislation than Feeney's Heath's Law. But it still has some bite. In fact, one could argue that it has the same bite as the formula with which Feeney himself has characterised the proper use of ancient literary criticism in the study of ancient literature: 'as an aid, even as a guide, but not as a prescription or a straitjacket.'[7] My one reservation is whether the antithesis articulated in this formula is sufficiently nuanced. Imagine me lost in an unfamiliar city. I ask someone the best way to my destination, and having listened to their directions I promptly wander off the opposite way. 'Here!' they exclaim, 'You're going the wrong way!' Would it make sense to retort that I wanted them to act as an aid, even as a guide, but not as a prescription or a straitjacket? A guide that never points us in a direction we would not otherwise have gone is superfluous. If we do not like the unexpected direction in which our guide points us, we may resent or resist the guidance; but if we are never willing to follow the prescription in such cases, there seems little point in having a guide at all. The application even of Heath's Heath's Law may sometimes

4. Contexts and consequences

confront us with the possibility that ancient literature was written to be read in unfamiliar, and perhaps even un-congenial, ways. If we are never willing to follow the prescription in such cases, there seems little point in claiming to use ancient criticism as a guide.

By way of illustration, it might be helpful to look at a specific interpretative question on which Feeney and I have disagreed. In *Unity in Greek Poetics* I argued that ancient criticism provides widespread and persistent evidence of a conception of literary unity different from the general approach most characteristic of modern criticism: 'where the characteristic tendency of modern criticism is to seek coherence in thematic unity, the characteristic tendency of ancient criticism was to seek coherence in thematic plurality ordered at a *formal* level.'[8] Consider, in this light, the remarkably complex and varied structure of Catullus 68b (that is, 68.41-160: I believe that lines 1-40 are a separate poem). This poem begins with a celebration of Allius' kindness to the poet: when he was in an agony of unfulfilled passion, Allius made available a house in which to meet his mistress (41-69). The mistress on her arrival at the threshold (70-2) is compared to Laodamia, arriving at the house of her husband Protesilaus (73f.) – a doomed marriage, since he was to die at Troy (75-90), where Catullus' own brother also died (91-100). This is the central point from which the poem moves backwards through the Trojan war (101-4) and Loadamia's love for her husband (105-30) to the comparison with Catullus' mistress (131-4), whose infidelities must be tolerated (135-42), not least because she is married not to Catullus but to another man (143-8) – and that leads us back to the celebration of Allius'

121

kindness (149-60). In a brief paper I once suggested (very sketchily) how the poem might be read in a way that accepts and celebrates its apparent proliferation of diverse themes and interests.[9] On this view, details such as the stark inconsistency between the lament for his brother (95, 'all our joys have died with you') and the celebration of his mistress (160, 'my light, whose life gives my life delight') can be understood as effects of the independent elaboration of motifs appropriate to two relatively autonomous local contexts. Catullus' artistry lay in the skilful management of formal transitions between contexts rather than in their thematic coordination.

My presentation of this case began by questioning the widespread view that the description of the mistress's arrival presents her as a bride or 'virtually' a bride. It pointed first to a number of confusions in the idea that the tableau of her dramatic pause in the doorway has any specifically bridal connotations; then it argued that, given the recognition of partial correspondence similes in ancient criticism, there is nothing inevitable about reading the comparison of the mistress's arrival to that of Laodamia as comparing them in respect of Laodamia's status as a bride. Feeney takes issue with this conclusion, asking pointedly whether I would 'maintain as stoutly that Gorgythion was not a poppy' (p. 222 n. 28); the reference is to the famous Homeric simile in which the dying Gorgythion 'dropped his head to one side like a poppy in a garden, bent by the weight of its seed and the showers of spring' (*Iliad* 8.306-8, tr. M. Hammond). The answer to Feeney's answer is, of course, that in the unlikely event of anyone trying to tell me that Gorgythion *was* a poppy, I would deny it. But since no one has tried to tell me that, there is no parallel to Catullus 68b, where interpreters *have* maintained that the mistress is a bride, or is 'virtually' a bride, or is like Laodamia in respect of her being a bride.

Naturally I do not deny that the mistress is like Laodamia in many respects; but in other respects she is unlike. Feeney himself maintains that 'it is the discrepancy, as much as the fit ... which generates much of the energy of the poem' (p. 37). Why, then, does he react so sharply to my highlighting of a particular discrepancy? The reason is that for his reading of the poem to work the reader must be unaware of this discrepancy at the point at which the simile is introduced. For Feeney, the discrepancy comes to light as the poem progresses from the mistress's arrival to the acknowledgement of her infidelities (p. 39):

> As the reader moves through these sixty lines, and their sequel, the discrepancy between the tenor and vehicle claims our attention as much as the match. The beloved is like and (finally) not like a bride, she is like and (finally) not like a goddess; the adulterous relationship between her and Catullus is like and (finally) not like a marriage.

This change in the reader's perception is necessary to secure an effect of temporary bafflement (p. 44):

> The reader's baffled experience in trying to follow the poet's words becomes a mirror of the poet's own baffled experience in trying to find words which will be adequate.

123

But a reader who has read 41-72 and correctly grasped the nature of the relationship between Catullus and the beloved would be strangely obtuse if, on reaching 'as in the past ablaze with love for her husband came Laodamia ...' (73f.), he says 'oh, yes, the beloved is just like a bride, isn't she!', and only later becomes gradually aware that she is not like a bride after all. To achieve the drama of discovery which his interpretation requires, Feeney offers us a reader whose readiness to be led by the nose is hard to reconcile with the alert sophistication that we normally find it convenient to posit in hypothetical readers of Catullus. That kind of reader would surely register from the start that, considered as a bride, Laodamia is not at all like the beloved. He is missing something crucial if he does not.

Moreover, if that sophisticated reader had been trained (as is likely) in rhetoric, he would find puzzling the difficulties Feeney's reader has with comparisons – for example, the crisis of faith occasioned by the discovery that one thing can be compared to two different things (p. 39), or the bafflement (p. 41) caused by what the rhetorically trained reader understands as a comparison of unequal objects designed for *amplificatio* (that is, the enhancement of the object of the comparison). Feeney is aware that, just as modern criticism has theorised 'the *dissimilarity* which is inherent in simile' on a conceptual level, so ancient rhetoric and criticism had theorised it on a technical level (p. 36). But he fails to use this information even as an aid or a guide. It is not integrated into his reading, which in consequence reaches conclusions that I believe lack historical plausibility. Likewise, I suggest, there are larger assumptions about the structure of poems in ancient criticism which can aid or guide us in grasping the possibility that the apparent proliferation of diverse and to some extent divergent themes in this poem is precisely that – and is nevertheless not a mistake or oversight on the poet's part.

To return to Feeney's formulation of the proper use of ancient criticism ('as an aid, even as a guide, but not as a prescription or a straitjacket'), my contention is that the concept of a guide cannot be divorced completely from that of prescription, since (as I suggested above) a guide whose prescriptions we always feel free to ignore is no guide at all. But this is not a recommendation of straitjackets. There is no implication that we are always obliged to follow a guide's prescription, or that we are ever obliged to follow it blindly. Guides sometimes prove unreliable, and there may be good reason for concluding in any given case that the guidance on offer should be rejected. The evidence of ancient reception must therefore be used critically, as must every kind of evidence. But critical use does not license uncritical rejection: to accord ancient reception prescriptive force is to say that we have to *work* for the conclusion that the evidence should, in a given case, be rejected.

Critical use implies selectivity, and that opens the way to a charge that the critic is simply picking out what he or she finds congenial. That charge risks circularity: to establish that a conclusion was reached because it was congenial, better evidence is needed than just the fact that it was reached. It might have been reached reluctantly, from a very different starting-point (see the case-studies in §4.1). Even establishing inconsistency on the part of the critic is not enough: although inconsistency may result from a capricious selection of the

Interpreting Classical Texts

congenial, it also may be the outcome of a struggle to accept uncongenial (or simply novel and unfamiliar) conclusions so severe that it was not carried through completely. I make these points by way of a plea in mitigation, since Feeney (p. 306) is unquestionably right in identifying one such failure in my *Poetics of Greek Tragedy*. In that book I documented the strand in ancient thinking about tragedy that emphasised its role as a source of (especially) moral teaching, and I acknowledged the importance of this idea – up to a point. I recruited it into my argument against the kind of intellectual preoccupations characteristic of modern approaches to tragedy, from which ancient didacticism is very different. But I made no attempt to integrate it into my understanding of the genre in any positive way. Neglecting the didactic view as a potentially positive component of tragedy's poetics was not a conclusion for which I had worked; there is no denying that in this case I simply shied away from an idea that seemed uncongenial and unproductive, and that this evasion introduced a serious flaw into the book's account of tragedy.[10]

I began the previous section by arguing that to accept the challenge posed by Aristodemus' seemingly bizarre theory about Homer was more productive than simply explaining it away. My flawed account of tragedy has now provided us with a cautionary illustration of the failure to take up the challenge posed by a seemingly uncongenial theme in ancient criticism. I conclude, therefore, with a formulation of the proper use of ancient literary criticism in the study of ancient literature that I prefer to Feeney's, even though I cannot claim consistently to have lived up to its demands: ancient criticism should

126

indeed be used as an aid and a guide, but it is even more important as a stimulus and a challenge.

4.5. Consequences

What, though, is the precise nature of that challenge? The project I have been describing looks towards a reconstruction of ancient conceptions of the function and structure of different kinds of text, with a view to using the reconstruction as an interpretative tool. Applied to texts that we treat as literature, this has been thought to imply an insistence 'that we think away the developments in esthetics that have shaped our own sensibilities as historical subjects'.[11] Since such self-erasure is obviously impossible, the project would thus be irretrievably discredited. But that is not what is at issue. The point is rather that my own historically shaped sensibilities are a contingent fact about myself from which no valid inference can be drawn when I am attempting to answer certain interpretative questions about ancient texts. I do not need to think those sensibilities away in order to discount them as evidence in the context of those enquiries. After all, though I cannot think away the peculiar personal resonance I find in Macbeth's description of the place where he meets the witches ('this blasted heath'), I am not remotely tempted to treat this contingent though inescapable fact about myself as relevant to the play's interpretation. If this seems too flippant, consider a case of greater existential import. Hymn-singing Helen (§2.3) does not imagine that her own theological convictions are relevant evidence when she pursues historical enquiries into the intended meaning of Newman's hymn or its contemporary reception; but this does not require her to forget her convictions or 'think them away'.

To become aware of the alien assumptions underlying classical literature, to understand them, and to appreciate their interpretative relevance does not require us to surrender anything that we already possess. On the contrary, in doing these things we *extend* our conceptual range. For example, it would hardly be controversial to say that the interpretation of a classical text requires us to understand and work with ancient assumptions about religion. If a Christian interpreter, less alert than Helen to the irrelevance of his own religious convictions, were to produce a reading of Greek tragedy in terms of sin, grace and redemption, we could not (as consistent pluralists) deny that his reading has value relative to some possible interest in the text; but we are unlikely to regard it as a successful contribution to classical scholarship. As classicists we expect the tragedy's religious content and implications to be explicated in terms of a model of ancient religious thought and practice. No one imagines that this entails our conversion to paganism. There is no assumption that reading classical literature in terms of ancient religion involves the surrender of our existing religious (or non-religious) beliefs. We acquire an additional repertoire of religious concepts, and learn to manipulate them; we read the classical texts by means of these concepts, but we are not at any risk of confusing them with the concepts we live by.

The study of the ancient world in general does not require us to surrender modern habits of thought and adopt ancient ones, about religion or anything else. Rather, we supplement our modern habits of thought by constructing models of ancient ways of thinking that we can use as the basis for further inference. This is not, in fact, something distinctive to the study of the ancient world. It is an extension of the development of perspectives on other people's perspectives that is essential to the construction of intersubjectivity typically involved in understanding others (§2.1). To make proper sense of a visiting friend's suggestion that we spend the day at Leeds Castle, I must attribute to her the belief that Leeds Castle is near my home in Leeds in Yorkshire; but I do not have to share the mistake myself, still less to think away my knowledge that Leeds Castle is hundreds of miles away in Kent. Gadamer, whose concept of the prejudicial structure of understanding we met in §4.1, has spoken of understanding as involving a 'fusion of horizons'. There is a sense in which the metaphor is misleading. We do not have access to two horizons. We inhabit one horizon, and the other is not available to us except as an interpretative construct, a model *within* our existing horizon. It is true, even so, that a horizon that does not embrace an appropriate model of the other's horizon cannot achieve understanding.

Another, more homely, image is that of allowing the text to speak in its own terms. This, too, is in one sense nonsensical. The text already speaks in its own terms; the interpreter's job is to render it intelligible to us by making it speak in our terms. Necessarily, therefore, the text as interpreted speaks in our terms, since the terms it speaks in are ones that we have supplied. But our stock of terms is not static: it changes as we change, and one of the things which can change us (and our stock of terms) is the activity of interpreting texts. In attempting to achieve a satisfactory explication of a text, we are likely to encounter the need to adapt and extend our existing conceptual repertoire – constructing (for example) hypothetical models of different ways in which people might think about gods, and testing them to see whether they help us to give a more coherent, comprehensive and economical account of the text in question. The interpreter's task of making the text speak in our terms may therefore be, in part, a matter of giving us new terms – not in place of the terms we had before, but in addition to them.

It may seem that I have been labouring the obvious in insisting that the reconstruction of ancient religious or ethical assumptions is an interpretatively useful extension of our conceptual range that does not require any kind of self-erasure on our part. Precisely so. How, then, are we to account for the anxiety aroused when the assumptions in question are ones to do with poetics (that is, assumptions concerning the structure and functions of literary or other texts)? Perhaps it is due in part to the very immediate link between poetics and the procedures of interpretation. A hypothesis about (for example) the kind of unity typically sought in ancient literary composition raises questions concerning the way we go about making sense of classical texts at a deeper level than does a hypothesis about ancient religious beliefs or ethical concepts. A hypothesis about ancient religion provides an additional datum to feed into our existing interpretative procedures; a hypothesis about ancient concepts of literary unity (if it is allowed to have interpretative relevance at all) may demand a change in our repertoire of interpretative procedures. How easy it is to slip into a tacit equation of familiar interpretative procedures with interpretation *per se* can be glimpsed in a quotation from Don Fowler which we have already considered in another context:[12]

> Moreover, the modernist classical critic is likely to find herself stabbed in the back by reception theorists like Malcolm Heath, who would deny that ancient readers would have felt this *need to interpret* which is the standard starting-point for accounts of ekphrasis.

But what is in question is not whether ancient readers would have felt 'this *need to interpret*'; it is whether they felt *this* need to interpret – that is, the one that Fowler's modernist critic assumes as her standard starting-point. My contention is that they may have interpreted differently; that is not the same as feeling no need to interpret. The implied equation of a particular interpretative strategy with interpretation as such is a subtle trap. I would argue, however, that it is precisely this intimate link between poetics and hermeneutic strategy which makes critical reflection on the possible distance between our own and ancient assumptions about poetics potentially so important for our engagement with classical texts.

Fowler goes on to deploy a variant of the objection cited at the start of this section when, seeking to 'deconstruct' the opposition between meaning and significance (cf. §2.4), he points out that 'the belief that one can ever free oneself from contemporary concerns is a delusion'.[13] I agree, of course. It should be obvious that freedom from contemporary concerns is not one of my aspirations. Without a contemporary concern there is no significance in the sense in which I use the term –

that is, no relation to an interest on the part of the interpreter, and hence no enquiry into meaning (or anything else). So I have, and could have, no desire to free myself from contemporary concerns. But a point made against Rorty in §3.4 is relevant here, too: one possible contemporary concern is a concern to achieve a historically informed understanding. And if that is a concern which one has, then the methodological implications have to be taken on board: a recognition (for example) that one's contemporary concerns may not be part of the body of evidence relevant to answering the questions one is asking; a recognition that one's own assumptions may be very different from those which underlay the composition of that text; and a willingness to invest effort in reconstructing the text's assumptions.

This reconstruction is, as I have already stressed, an extension of our conceptual range. Successful interpretation does not in itself change the way I think about the world, but will sometimes open my eyes to other ways in which the world has been thought of. It is here that we encounter the potential gain from listening to others that we noted in §3.4. Coming to understand other ways in which the world has been thought about may bring to light other ways in which we could think about the world; and that in turn may change the ways in which we do think about the world.

We are no longer concerned here with interpretation, but with its indirect consequences for the interpreter. These consequences are not answerable to the text, and are not subject to the constraints of historical enquiry. Indeed, the greater the cultural distance of the text in question, the less meaningful it is to think of these consequences in terms of a simple appropriation of the concepts developed to make sense of it. Just as Aristodemus' theory about Homer is unavailable to us (as we saw in §1.2, the change in background assumptions means that if we were to say what Aristodemus said we would in fact be saying something different), so too are the religious beliefs of archaic Greeks. Trying to understand the *Oresteia* decisively changed the course of my own thinking in philosophy and theology, but this was not because I adopted archaic Greek ways of conceiving divine causality and human responsibility (that would have made no sense). Rather, reflection on archaic Greek conceptions enlarged my understanding of the range of ways in which such matters could be thought about, and that in turn changed my relationship to the resources available within the philosophical and theological traditions that constituted the context of my own thinking.

A parallel process is possible within the sphere of aesthetics. To understand alien literary texts we may need to understand an alien literary aesthetic. But that, I have argued, places a strictly limited demand on us: we need to model the alien aesthetic, not to adopt it as our own. In all probability, we *could* not adopt it as our own: we can make no more sense of the notion of a modern reader experiencing Greek tragedy as Greek audiences experienced it than we can of a modern reader sharing an archaic Greek's religious beliefs. But the encounter with an alien aesthetic may nevertheless have some impact on our own aesthetics. For there is no reason to think of aesthetic sensibility as something formed once and fixed forever; what has been formed may be transformed by new experience and reflection. To be sure, there is no reason why we should feel bound to follow the lead of the alien aesthetic beyond the confines of our historical research. The conclusions we reach in historical enquiry place no obligations on us outside that context. We are free to misread as strongly as we choose. But why should we not *also* take the opportunity to explore new possibilities for the appreciation of literature? We have nothing to lose but the constraints of familiarity.

Notes

1. Interpretation and dissent

1. On errors of judgement in tragedy see above all Aristotle, *Poetics* 13 and 14. My view of *Antigone* is briefly sketched out in M. Heath, *The Poetics of Greek Tragedy* (London: Duckworth, 1987), 73-7 (but I would not necessarily now agree with everything that I wrote then). For some alternative views see (e.g.): C. Sourvinou-Inwood, 'Assumptions and the creation of meaning: reading Sophocles' *Antigone*', *Journal of Hellenic Studies* 109 (1989), 134-48; P. Holt, 'Polis and tragedy in the *Antigone*', *Mnemosyne* 52 (1999), 658-90.

2. R. Rorty, 'Deconstruction', in R. Selden (ed.), *Cambridge History of Literary Criticism*, vol. 8: *From Formalism to Poststructuralism* (Cambridge: Cambridge University Press, 1995), 166-96, p. 168.

3. D. Fowler, *Roman Constructions* (Oxford: Oxford University Press, 2000), 13. This paper ('Postmodernism, romantic irony, and classical closure') was first published in I.J.F. de Jong and J.P. Sullivan (ed.), *Modern Critical Theory and Classical Texts* (*Mnemosyne* Suppl. 130, Leiden: Brill, 1994), 231-56.

4. M. Heath, 'Longinus *On Sublimity*', *Proceedings of the Cambridge Philological Society* 45 (1999), 43-74.

5. *Roman Constructions*, vii. The sentence continues, '... and our constructions are not part of a disinterested pursuit of the truth about the past but part of our dialogue with contemporaries', which skews an already gratuitous antithesis by attaching the equally gratuitous 'disinterested' to one side.

6. For some of the reasons why Aristodemus' suggestion was not, in its own context, crazy, see §4.3 below.

7. On this change of mind see further §4.1 below. For some early contributions to the debate see: M. Lefkowitz, 'Who sang Pindar's victory odes?', *American Journal of Philology* 109 (1988), 1-11; M. Heath, 'Receiving the κῶμος: the context and performance of epinician', *American Journal of Philology* 109 (1988), 180-95; A. Burnett, 'Performing Pindar's odes', *Classical Philology* 84 (1989), 283-93; C. Carey, 'The performance of the victory ode', *American Journal of Philology* 110 (1989), 545-65; M. Heath and M. Lefkowitz, 'Epinician performance: a response to Burnett and Carey', *Classical Philology* 86 (1991), 173-91. The Lefkowitz-Heath view (that the traditional assumption that epinician was choral is not well-founded, and that there are positive reasons for entertaining the alternative hypothesis that epinician was or might sometimes have been composed for solo performance) has met with some support, but remains a minority opinion.

2. Variety in interpretation

1. The example is borrowed from Don Fowler, who comments: 'No amount of wishing on my part will make the

phrase "I like cats for breakfast" allude to my aunt Mabel, whatever is happening inside my head when I utter the sentence.' See D. Fowler, *Roman Constructions* (Oxford: Oxford University Press, 2000), 118. This paper ('On the shoulders of giants: intertextuality and classical studies') was first published in *Materiali e discussioni* 39 (1997), 13-34.

2. E.D. Hirsch, *The Aims of Interpretation* (Chicago: University of Chicago Press, 1976), 2f.

3. D. Fowler, *Roman Constructions*, 70. This paper ('Narrate and describe: the problem of ekphrasis') was first published in *Journal of Roman Studies* 81 (1991), 25-35.

4. M. Heath, *Unity in Greek Poetics* (Oxford: Clarendon Press, 1989), 155.

3. Good intentions

1. E.D. Hirsch, *Validity in Interpretation* (New Haven: Yale University Press, 1967), 21; cf. 22, 48f., 51-4, 221, 223. Having said that much on Hirsch's behalf, I must emphasise that his theory of intention and meaning differs in many important respects from the one I am defending here.

2. See Further Reading (3a).

3. R.O.A.M. Lyne, 'Vergil's *Aeneid*: subversion by intertextuality. Catullus 66.39-40 and other examples', *Greece and Rome* 41 (1994), 187-204, p. 189 (original emphasis).

4. L. Edmunds, introducing P. Culham and L. Edmunds (ed.), *Classics: a discipline and profession in crisis?* (Lanham: University Press of America, 1989), xxii.

5. See P. Light, 'Context, conservation and conversation', in M. Richards and P. Light (ed.), *Children of Social Worlds*

(Cambridge, MA: Harvard University Press, 1986), 170-90; K. Hundeide, 'The message structure of some Piagetian experiments', in Astri Heen Wold (ed.), *The Dialogical Alternative: towards a theory of language and mind* (Oslo: Scandinavian University Press, 1992), 139-56.

6. R.G. Williams, 'I shall be spoken: textual boundaries, authors, and intention', in G. Bornstein and R.G. Williams (ed.), *Palimpsest: editorial theory in the humanities* (Ann Arbor 1993), 45-64, p. 58.

7. S. Hinds, *Allusion and Intertext* (Cambridge: Cambridge University Press, 1998), 47f. (original emphasis).

8. The complex debate on the date of the Egesta decree can be pursued backwards from A. Henry, 'Pour encourager les autres: Athens and Egesta encore', *Classical Quarterly* 45 (1995), 232-40; S.E. Dawson, 'The Egesta decree: *IG* I^3 11', *Zeitschrift für Papyrologie und Epigraphik* 112 (1996), 248-52. Possible broader consequences if the later dating is accepted: H. Mattingly, 'Epigraphy and the Athenian empire', *Historia* 41 (1992), 129-38, and *The Athenian Empire Restored* (Ann Arbor: University of Michigan Press, 1996).

9. This (unavoidably schematic) discussion has drawn on M. Heath, *The Poetics of Greek Tragedy* (London: Duckworth, 1987), and 'Sophocles *Philoctetes*: a problem play?', in J. Griffin (ed.), *Sophocles Revisited: essays in honour of Hugh Lloyd-Jones* (Oxford: Oxford University Press, 1999), 137-60. The book argues for (b); the paper offers some clarifications of the book's project, along with an acknowledgement that the failure to give due weight to (c) was a major flaw in its execution of that project.

10. E.g. E.D. Hirsch, *Validity in Interpretation* (New Ha-

ven: Yale University Press, 1967), 5f.: 'If the meaning of a text is not the author's, then no interpretation can possibly correspond to *the* meaning of the text, since the text can have no determinate or determinable meaning .... If a theorist wants to save the ideal of validity he has to save the author as well.'

11. R. Rorty, *Consequences of Pragmatism* (Minneapolis: University of Minneapolis Press, 1982), 151. This paper ('Nineteenth-century idealism and twentieth-century textualism') was first published in *The Monist* 64 (1981), 155-74.

12. *Consequences of Pragmatism*, 86f. This paper ('Texts and lumps: philosophy of science and literary theory') was first published in *New Literary History* 17 (1985), 1-16.

4. Contexts and consequences

1. For the (interim!) end point of this change of perspective, see M. Heath, *Political Comedy in Aristophanes* (*Hypomnemata* 87, Göttingen: Vandenhoeck & Ruprecht, 1987) (agon of *Wasps*: 38-40; ideological tension: 35f.; democratic control: 42f.; *Frogs* parabasis: 19-21). Since this was my first publication on Aristophanes, the extent to which it was an exercise in self-criticism has naturally not been obvious to readers. Subsequent reflections in M. Heath, 'Aristophanes and the discourse of politics', in G. Dobrov (ed.), *The City as Comedy* (Chapel Hill: University of North Carolina Press, 1997), 230-49.

2. For the debate on the performance of epinician see ch. 1 n. 7; the book review mentioned in the text is in *Classical Review* 35 (1985), 178-9. For the conventional view of encomiastic futures see (e.g.) W.J. Slater, 'Futures in Pindar',

Classical Quarterly 19 (1969), 86-94; I.J. Pfeiffer, *First Person Futures in Pindar* (*Hermes* Einzelschriften 81, Munich: Franz Steiner Verlag, 1999) has now made a strong case that they are unnecessary even on the choral hypothesis. Pfeiffer's arguments against the solo hypothesis (p. 38f. n. 49) were mostly already addressed by Lefkowitz and myself in our response to Burnett and Carey. His description of my approach as making a 'sharp distinction' between *kômoi* and formal epinician songs illustrates how difficult it can be to adjust to a different perspective: I see my approach as establishing a *close integration* of the commissioned epinician into the *kômos* that was its performance context.

3. H.-G. Gadamer, *Philosophical Hermeneutics* (Berkeley: University of California Press, 1976), 9: 'It is not so much our judgements [*Urteile*] as it is our prejudices [*Vorurteile*] that constitute our being .... The historicity of our existence entails that prejudices, in the literal sense of the word, constitute the initial directedness of our whole ability to experience. Prejudices are biases of our openness to the world.' See Further Reading (4a).

4. More detailed discussion in M. Heath, 'Was Homer a Roman?', *Papers of the Leeds International Latin Seminar* 10 (1998), 23-56.

5. Aristotle and errors: see ch. 1 n. 1. Rhetoricians and intentional ambiguity: Richard F. Thomas, *Virgil and the Augustan Reception* (Cambridge: Cambridge University Press, 2001), 1, 7-11.

6. D. Feeney, 'Criticism ancient and modern', in D. Innes, H. Hine and C. Pelling (ed.), *Ethics and Rhetoric: classical essays for Donald Russell on his seventy-fifth birthday* (Ox-

ford: Clarendon Press, 1995), 301-12, p. 303. The passage which Feeney cites in support of this attribution is from M. Heath, *The Poetics of Greek Tragedy* (London: Duckworth, 1987), 3.

7. D. Feeney, *The Gods in Epic: poets and critics of the classical tradition* (Oxford: Clarendon Press, 1991), 3, quoted in 'Criticism ancient and modern', p. 302.

8. M. Heath, *Unity in Greek Poetics* (Oxford: Clarendon Press, 1989), 150 (by 'modern' here I mean that the tendency in question became dominant from the eighteenth century onwards: this thesis about ancient poetics is linked to investigations in the history of reception of the kind discussed in §4.2).

9. M. Heath, 'Catullus 68b', *Liverpool Classical Monthly* 13 (1988), 117-19, with the response in D.C. Feeney, ' "Shall I compare thee ...?" Catullus 68b and the limits of analogy', in A.J. Woodman and J. Powell (ed.), *Authors and Audience* (Cambridge: Cambridge University Press, 1992), 33-44, with 220-4 (notes).

10. See M. Heath, 'Sophocles *Philoctetes*: a problem play?', in J. Griffin (ed.), *Sophocles Revisited: essays in honour of Hugh Lloyd-Jones* (Oxford: Oxford University Press, 1999), 137-60; above, ch. 3 n. 9. It is of course another question – to which I do not yet have a clear answer – just how the flaw should be remedied. It is one thing to recognise that relevant evidence has not been taken seriously enough, but quite another to determine what conclusions are to be drawn from it. Those conclusions, too, have to be worked for.

11. R. Lamberton, reviewing *Unity in Greek Poetics* in *Ancient Philosophy* 11 (1991), 465-73, p. 472.

12. D. Fowler, *Roman Constructions* (Oxford: Oxford University Press, 2000), 70 (from 'Narrate and describe': see above, ch. 2 n. 3).

13. *Roman Constructions*, 70f.

Further Reading

1. Interpretation and dissent

(a) On the importance of disagreement see Nicholas Rescher, *Pluralism: against the demand for consensus* (Oxford: Clarendon Press, 1993), and the discussion of 'objectivity' in Mark Bevir, *The Logic of the History of Ideas* (Cambridge: Cambridge University Press, 1999), 78-126 (p. 103: 'We make better and better sense of the world through a continuous process of dialectical competition between rival webs of theories which themselves are being constantly modified and extended'). The case studies in Richard F. Hamilton, *The Social Misconstruction of Reality: validity and verification in the scholarly community* (New Haven: Yale University Press, 1996) illustrate the dangers of uncritically sustained consensus.

(b) The philosophical basis of my approach is most indebted to pragmatism, and in particular to the strand of the pragmatist tradition that goes back to C.S. Peirce. Peirce's contribution to semiotics has often been cited by literary theorists, but I have found more stimulus in his thinking about truth and enquiry. W.B. Gallie, *Peirce and Pragmatism* (Harmondsworth: Penguin, 1952) remains a useful and accessible

introduction. For explorations of the potential of Peirce's
thought (and some of its many problems) see Cheryl J. Misak,
Truth and the End of Inquiry: a Peircean account of truth
(Oxford: Clarendon Press, 1991); Christopher Hookway,
Truth, Rationality and Pragmatism: themes from Peirce (Ox-
ford: Oxford University Press, 2000). Recent attempts to
develop this strand of pragmatism include: Nicholas Rescher,
*Methodological Pragmatism: a systems-theoretic approach to
the theory of knowledge* (Oxford: Blackwell, 1977), *Empirical
Inquiry* (Totowa: Rowman & Littlefield, 1982), and *Inquiry
Dynamics* (New Brunswick: Transaction, 2000); Susan Haack,
Evidence and Inquiry: towards reconstruction in epistemology
(Oxford: Blackwell, 1993). Karl-Otto Apel combines Peircean
themes with perspectives drawn from modern German phi-
losophy in works such as *From a Transcendental-Semiotic
Point of View* (Manchester: Manchester University Press,
1998) – not an easy read, despite the catchy title.

(c) Another important philosophical stimulus has come
from certain aspects of the work of Donald Davidson (see also
2(f)); see, in particular, the collections *Inquiries into Truth and
Interpretation* (ed. 2, Oxford: Oxford University Press, 2001),
and *Subjective, Intersubjective, Objective* (Oxford: Oxford
University Press, 2001), and *Truth, Language and History*
(Oxford: Oxford University Press, forthcoming). There are
good discussions in B.T. Ramberg, *Donald Davidson's Philosophy of Language: an introduction* (Oxford: Blackwell, 1989)
and J.E. Malpas, *Donald Davidson and the Mirror of Meaning:
holism, truth, interpretation* (Cambridge: Cambridge University Press, 1992); both explore connections between Davidson
and Gadamer (see 4(a)). For a relevant collection of essays see

R.W. Dasenbrock (ed.), *Literary Theory after Davidson* (University Park: Pennyslvania University Press, 1993).

(d) One thing that used to puzzle me about Richard Rorty is how a philosopher so heavily indebted to Davidson could continue to maintain certain characteristic dualisms (exhortations to see 'sentences as connected with other sentences *rather than* with the world', and so on). Rorty himself has now come to acknowledge the problem: see his 'Response to Bjørn Ramberg', in R.B. Brandom (ed.), *Rorty and his Critics* (Oxford: Blackwell, 2000), 370-7 (p. 375: 'Ramberg has persuaded me to abandon two doctrines which I have been preaching for years: that the notion of "getting things right" must be abandoned, and that "true of" and "refers to" are not word-world relations'). This retraction has relevance to the points I make in §1.4 on the false opposition between discovery and construction, and to my comments on 'getting it right' in §3.4. The essays and replies in Brandom's collection provide a good idea of how Rorty's thought is situated in the current philosophical context.

(e) The importance of tacit skills, and the distinction between attending to and attending from, derive from Michael Polanyi, *Personal Knowledge: towards a post-critical philosophy* (London: Routledge, 1959), and *The Tacit Dimension* (London: Routledge, 1967).

2. Variety in interpretation

(a) The chapter-title alludes to, and signals my dissent from, E.D. Hirsch, *Validity in Interpretation* (New Haven: Yale University Press, 1967). This book, and Hirsch's *The Aims of*

145

Interpretation (Chicago: University of Chicago Press, 1976), present a classic, but strongly anti-pluralist, defence of intentionalism (see 3(a)).

(b) The pluralist view of 'meaning' and 'interpretation' taken in this chapter is close to that of Jeffrey Stout, 'What is the meaning of a text?', *New Literary History* 14 (1982/3), 1-12, and 'The relativity of interpretation', *The Monist* 69 (1986), 103-18.

(c) My thinking about language and meaning has been influenced by, or discovered congenial convergences with, a number of different authors. The school of linguistic theory known as 'systemic linguistics', associated in particular with M.A.K. Halliday, is the source of the abstract model of language that I have found the most helpful, in particular because of its strong emphasis on social and functional aspects of language, and on language as meaning-potential. See M.A.K. Halliday, *Language as Social Semiotic: the social interpretation of language and meaning* (London: Edward Arnold, 1978), and *Learning How to Mean: explorations in the development of language* (London: Edward Arnold, 1975); Christopher Butler, *Systemic Linguistics: theory and applications* (London: Batsford, 1985). See also 4(d).

(d) However, all theoretical frameworks for the description of language as system or structure (the Saussurean *langue*), precisely because of the methodologically necessary abstraction from the concrete realities of linguistic behaviour, have the potential to distort our vision. The forceful critique of Saussure's 'abstract objectivism' in Valentin Vološinov, *Marxism and the Philosophy of Language* (London: Seminar Press, 1973) is particularly valuable here.

(e) The work of Donald Davidson is also relevant: see especially 'A nice derangement of epitaphs', in E. Lepore (ed.), *Truth and Interpretation: perspectives on the philosophy of Donald Davidson* (Oxford: Blackwell, 1986), 433-46 (p. 446: 'there is no such thing as a language, not if a language is anything like what many philosophers and linguists have supposed'), and 'The social aspect of language', in B. McGuinness and G. Olivieri (ed.), *The Philosophy of Michael Dummett* (Dordrecht: Huwer, 1994), 1-16. Both papers are reprinted in *Truth, Language and History* (see 1(c)).

(f) Another important influence has been the work of the social psychologist Ragnar Rommetveit on the dialogical construction of intersubjectivity: see especially *On Message Structure: a framework for the study of language and communication* (London: John Wiley, 1974). For a collection of more recent work influenced by Rommetveit's dialogical and social-cognitive approach, see Astri Heen Wold (ed.), *The Dialogical Alternative: towards a theory of language and mind* (Oslo: Scandinavian University Press, 1992); the title reflects the affinity between Rommetveit's approach and Bakhtin. There is an interview with Rommetveit, with a selective bibliography including references to more recent publications, in Ingrid E. Josephs, 'Do you know Ragnar Rommetveit?', *Culture and Psychology* 4 (1998), 189-212.

(g) Complementary insights are provided from a different perspective by Dan Sperber and Deirdre Wilson, *Relevance: communication and cognition* (ed. 2, Oxford: Blackwell 1995) (p. 193: 'We see communication as a matter of enlarging mutual cognitive environments, not of duplicating thoughts').

3. Good intentions

(a) In Anglo-American criticism impetus was given to the discussion of authorial intention by W.K. Wimsatt and M.C. Beardsley, 'The intentional fallacy', first published in *Sewanee Review* 54 (1946), 468-88, and often reprinted in more accessible locations: see (e.g.) W.K. Wimsatt, *The Verbal Icon: studies in the meaning of poetry* (Lexington: University of Kentucky Press, 1954), 3-18, or D. Newton-De Molina (ed.), *On Literary Intention: critical essays* (Edinburgh: Edinburgh University Press, 1976), 1-13. Newton-De Molina collects a number of papers on the debate that arose out of Wimsatt and Beardsley and Hirsch's defence of intentionalism (see 2(a)); see also G. Iseminger (ed.), *Intention and Interpretation* (Philadelphia: Temple University Press, 1992). S. Burke, *The Death and Return of the Author: criticism and subjectivity in Barthes, Foucault and Derrida* (Edinburgh: Edinburgh University Press, 1992) provides a discussion of how the problem has been handled in a different tradition.

(b) There is an interesting discussion of interpretation and intention from a different disciplinary perspective in Mark Bevir, *The Logic of the History of Ideas* (Cambridge: Cambridge University Press, 1999), 31-77. However, I think the continuation (129-42) illustrates the pointlessness of framing the issue in terms of the meaning of 'meaning', rather than of the delimitation of the questions relevant to a particular context of enquiry.

(c) Theorists of textual criticism have also given considerable attention to the status of authorial intention (without, of course, reaching a consensus). For a useful survey of recent work on the theory of textual criticism (from a perspective with which I have much sympathy) see G.T. Tanselle, 'Textual instability and editorial idealism', *Studies in Bibliography* 49 (1996), 1-60. It should be noted, however, that the issues confronting editors of modern texts are not identical to those posed by classical texts.

(d) For the approach to language that underlies the discussion in this chapter see the references given under 2(c)-(g). On the opacity of the concept of consciousness see K. Wilkes, 'Is consciousness important?', *British Journal of the Philosophy of Science* 35 (1984), 233-42.

4. Contexts and consequences

(a) For the critique of 'the prejudice against prejudice' and the idea of a 'fusion of horizons' see Hans-Georg Gadamer, *Truth and Method* (ed. 2, revised by Joel Weinsheimer and Donald G. Marshall, London: Sheed and Ward, 1989). My appropriation of themes from Gadamer's hermeneutics goes along with resistance to many of the things that Gadamer himself does with them. Georgia Warnke, *Gadamer: hermeneutics, tradition and reason* (London: Polity Press, 1987) provides a good introduction, with a sympathetic but probing examination of some of the tensions and obscurities in Gadamer's thought. See also 1(c).

(b) For a general overview of trends in reception-oriented criticism see R.C. Holub, *Reception Theory: a critical introduction* (London: Methuen, 1984). One important contribution is Hans-Robert Jauss, *Toward an Aesthetics of*

Reception (Brighton: Harvester, 1982). There is an excellent critical discussion of Jauss in R.R. Nauta, 'Historicizing reading: the aesthetics of reception and Horace's "Soracte Ode" ', in I.J.F. de Jong and J.P. Sullivan (ed.) *Modern Critical Theory and Classical Texts* (*Mnemosyne* Suppl. 130, Leiden: Brill, 1994), 207-30.

(c) My own essays in the modern history of reception can be found in M. Heath, 'The origins of modern Pindaric criticism', *Journal of Hellenic Studies* 106 (1986), 85-98; ' "Jure principem locum tenet": Euripides' *Hecuba*', *Bulletin of the Institute of Classical Studies* 34 (1987), 40-68 (revised and abbreviated in J. Mossman (ed.), *Oxford Readings in Euripides* (Oxford: Oxford University Press, 2002)); and *Unity in Greek Poetics* (Oxford: Clarendon Press, 1989), 137-49. For an excellent recent example of the use of reception-history see Richard F. Thomas, *Virgil and the Augustan Reception* (Cambridge: Cambridge University Press, 2001).

(d) The distinction between 'context of culture' and 'context of situation' is adapted from systemic linguistics. Similarly, the concept of genre as a set of resources for realising choices from a structured but open-ended system of meaning-potential within a shared linguistic practice draws on the systemic concept of 'register'. See 2(c), and M. Gregory and S. Carroll, *Language and Situation: language varieties and their social contexts* (London: Routledge, 1978).

Index

Index